THE BABY SWAP CONSPIRACY

THE
Baby Swap
CONSPIRACY

**THE SHOCKING TRUTH
BEHIND THE FLORIDA
CASE OF TWO BABIES
SWITCHED AT BIRTH**

LORETTA SCHWARTZ-NOBEL

VILLARD BOOKS
NEW YORK
1993

Grateful acknowledgment is made to the following for permission to reprint
previously published material:

DWARF MUSIC: Excerpt from the lyrics of "I Shall Be Released" by Bob Dylan.
Copyright © 1967, 1970 by Dwarf Music (ASCAP). Reprinted by permission of
Dwarf Music. All rights reserved. International copyright secured.

EDITE KROLL LITERARY AGENCY: Excerpt from "The Network of the Imaginary Mother"
from *The Lady of the Beasts* by Robin Morgan. © 1962, 1968, 1973, 1974, 1975, 1976 by
Robin Morgan. Reprinted by permission of Edite Kroll Literary Agency.

Library of Congress Cataloging-in-Publication Data
Schwartz-Nobel, Loretta.
Baby swap: the shocking truth behind the Florida case of two babies
switched at birth/Loretta Schwartz-Nobel.—1st ed.
p.   cm.
ISBN 0-679-40015-X
1. Infants switched at birth.   2. Mays family.   3. Twigg family.
4. Custody of children.   I. Title.
RJ253.S39   1992
362.82'97—dc20   91-41273

9   8   7   6   5   4   3   2

First Edition

To the memory of Arlena
To the lost days with Kimberly
and to Irisa, Normia, Gina, Will,
Tommy and Barry, whose suffering
has too often been forgotten

There is a time to separate from our mother
But unless we are ready to separate
Unless we are ready to leave her and be left
Anything is better than separation.

—Judith Viorst

Acknowledgments

I am grateful for the countless number of hours that Regina Twigg, Ernest Twigg, the Twigg children, Cindy Tanner Mays and John Blakely have spent with me.

This book could not have been written without the help and support of my husband, Joel Nobel. I also want to thank my typist, Claudia Disu; my mother, Fay Rosenberg; my daughters, Ruth and Rebecca; and our baby-sitter, Rosemary Gross, who has been a second mother to my young son, Adam, during all the hours I spent writing.

My deepest gratitude to my agent, Ellen Levine, and my editor, Diane Reverand, whose confidence and skill helped make this book a reality.

Contents

Contents

Contents

PART VI EPILOGUE 227

A Note of Explanation

The voices of Regina Twigg and Cindy Mays are taken from taped interviews with them, which have been edited for clarity.

Certain scenes and portions of dialogue in this book have been dramatically re-created on the basis of interviews and transcripts and presented chronologically. Where scenes and dialogue are based on the recollection of people being interviewed, they may reflect the perspectives of those people. It is impossible to reconstruct these events and conversations perfectly, but I have tried to be as accurate as possible.

Introduction

Like so many others, I first learned about this case from a newspaper article. I had no particular bias, no opinions about the people involved, no theories about how the switch had occurred. As a mother myself, I responded to the horror of a parent's nightmare. I was also an investigative journalist interested in learning as much as I could. For several weeks I clipped and studied everything I saw on the subject.

There was something about the intensity of Regina Twigg's face, even in the blurry newspaper clippings, that kept calling me back. In the weeks that followed, I wrote a book proposal, found a publisher, and signed a contract.

It wasn't as easy as I had hoped. On her lawyer John Blakely's advice, Regina Twigg could not talk to me for more than a year. Robert Mays also refused. There had been no trial, no significant public record, and without their help there could be no book. I put the project on hold and waited.

Finally I received a call from John Blakely. He and the

Twiggs were interviewing potential authors and wanted me to fly down to Florida. I took my place in a lineup of hungry journalists and filmmakers. When I met Regina and Ernest Twigg and their two attorneys in a large conference room, I made it clear that this would be my project. If they worked with me, I alone would have to determine the direction that the book took. That direction was still unknown. They agreed.

As it turned out the process was more complex than I anticipated. The more I spoke with Regina the more I began to wonder about the life of the child Regina had given birth to, who had grown up in another city with another family. I called Bob Mays's attorney again and left messages. Mays never returned my calls. Later I learned that he had his own book proposal making the rounds of New York publishers. He was working with an author from Texas who had put together "an excellent package" about the death of Bob Mays's first wife, Barbara, and the love between the lonely widower and his only child. It never became a book. It did, however, become part of the NBC miniseries called *Switched at Birth*. The miniseries was seen by twenty million viewers. I was one of them, but I wanted to know more.

The only other person with intimate knowledge of the life of Kimberly Mays was Cindy Tanner Mays, the woman Bob married after his first wife's death—the woman who had raised Kimberly and been her psychological mother from the time she was two years old.

For five months I called Cindy and her attorneys. Each time I was told that since her divorce from Bob Mays she had put that part of her life behind her and did not want to get involved. Finally, I said, "Cindy, I know you have information that no one else has—essential information that would help the Twiggs determine what is really in Kimberly's best interest. If you love her you should come forward."

"I do love her, very much, and you're right," she said. "I'll do it."

I flew to Tampa the next morning. We met in the Radisson Bay Hotel and spent the next three days and nights talking, stopping only long enough to sleep and eat.

The story that emerged was shockingly different from what I had expected. Shockingly different from the story of the lonely widower and fine single parent that the press and miniseries had portrayed. Smooth, charming and affable on one level, Bob Mays now appeared to be controlling, explosive and abusive on another.

I have presented the story Cindy Tanner Mays told me in her own words without comment, only after it was substantiated by the depositions of psychiatrists and psychologists who knew and worked with the Mays family at that time. Bob Mays's attorney claims that Cindy is a vindictive ex-wife and denies that Mays ever abused Kimberly.

Far from being a vindictive ex-wife, I found Cindy Mays to be a protective one. For more than two years she had remained silent, even when asked to comment by reporters who knew her well. Since Cindy worked as the public relations news and media person for the Tampa General Hospital, there were a lot of those reporters. I was the only one she chose to trust.

Cindy took me into the home that Bob and Kimberly had lived in. She shared her treasured photographs and memories. She allowed me to speak with her daughter Ashlee, who had been raised as Kimberly's sister.

What ultimately emerged were the stories of both Kimberly Mays and Arlena Twigg, two little girls switched at birth who never knew each other, and two women, also unknown to each other, Regina Twigg and Cindy Mays, each raising and loving daughters who were not their own. Two women who valued family above all else. Two women who, ironically, both lost the little girls they loved at the age of nine. Both women told stories of remarkably beautiful children, brave children, struggling against loss after loss. I have tried to re-create their stories, their dreams, and their longings as accurately as possible. I have tried to examine the forces that shaped those dreams and propelled their lives.

The more I learned, the more I found myself wondering what had really happened more than a decade before in that small Florida hospital. I found myself being drawn into a tangled web of unanswered questions, altered documents, conveniently faulty memories and overt lies. I traveled to Florida and visited Hardee Memorial Hospital without revealing my identity. I gained access to long-buried documents and to private investigators' reports.

I spent countless hours poring over hospital charts, nurses' notes, altered birth certificates and volumes of depositions that often contradicted each other. What evolved was far more explosive than I had ever imagined.

For more than three years, I not only followed the case, I lived it. Sometimes it took me to places I'd rather not have gone, but by this time I had no choice. I had to know. Along with the stories of the children and the revelations about Bob Mays, I had to try to unravel the missing pieces of the baby swap conspiracy that had led to so much pain, to so much loss and, inadvertently, to such remarkable stories of love and courage, the stories of Arlena Twigg and Kimberly Mays.

—Loretta Schwartz-Nobel
Philadelphia, Pennsylvania

Part 1

DAUGHTERS

We first see the
world through
the eyes of a
little child, and
that inner child
remains with us
throughout our
lives no matter
how outwardly
grown up and
powerful we
become.

JOHN BRADSHAW

The Voice of
Regina Twigg

Someone was pushing us into the back of a car, onto the floorboards, shoving us down, holding our heads so we wouldn't see the police dragging her off. It was a big, black, shiny car. The windows were closed. It was a warm summer day and it was hot in the car, and their breath was hot and sour. They held us down behind the seats so that we wouldn't see her or hear her screaming and crying for her children. But somehow I did see her and hear her, and I remember to this day the terror that I felt. I was three years old and she was my mother.

First a relative had us. She beat my little sisters with a belt if they didn't perform on the potty the second she told them to. The state took us away from her because she was not sending us to school. That's when we were placed in the orphanage.

Two or three times my mother was brought to the orphanage from the mental institution by the department of social services to see us. I remember that she kissed us and talked to us and bought us candy, and that she wept and clung to us and said, "I love you. I'll always love you," when she had to leave.

Then one day we were told that she was dead and that they were going to put us up for adoption. Years later I learned that they told her she would never get out of there to raise us. They convinced her that it was best for us if she signed the adoption papers. She wanted us to have some kind of a chance for a normal home and life, so she signed the papers.

All I could do my entire childhood, whenever I was hurt or sad or lonely, was to remember how she rocked me in her arms in a rocking chair and sang lullabies to me.

Chapter 1

The Switch

By eleven o'clock on the night of December 2, 1978, Regina Twigg knew it was time. The nagging cramps that began in the small of her back had moved to her belly and had become sharper and more regular. The fact that this was her seventh baby didn't make it any easier or less frightening. Especially since Vivia, her last baby girl, had died suddenly at the age of six weeks.

Regina knew you could never be grateful enough for a healthy baby, or too careful about choosing good medical care. That's why this time she had selected Dr. William Black and Hardee Memorial Hospital. Her friend Celia Warrington had recommended it, even though the hospital was nearly an hour's drive from her house.

"Ernest," Regina said, "I think it's going to be quick." Ernest glanced up from the TV and yawned. Regina knew it was a deceptive calm and that her husband kept all the tension inside, where it ate away at him. Still, he steadied her. She double-checked her already-packed hospital bag and glanced back at Ernest. He was smiling. The lines in his face deepened and crinkled around his eyes. "Good ole Ernest," she laughed. "Still truckin' along as if we had all night." The truth was that she trusted him to get her there on time, or to deliver the baby himself if he had to. He was more stable than anything she had ever known in her entire life. At some level, she believed he could do anything.

Ernest stood up, shuffled over and patted Regina on the back. He winked at Meta, the seventy-eight-year-old German woman who lived in the little yellow cottage behind them. Meta had arrived only minutes after Regina's first contraction and excited phone call. Regina hesitated, her green eyes darting around the room for any last-minute things she might have forgotten.

At thirty-five, she was a striking woman with strawberry blond hair, high cheekbones, a patrician nose, flawless pink skin and perfect white teeth. Little in her appearance, except perhaps the piercing intensity of her eyes, belied the tragedy of her early life.

Regina walked with the heavy, lumbering gait of late pregnancy through the narrow hallway toward her oldest daughter's room. At ten, Irisa was already a little mother, caring for the family. She hovered over the younger children and sometimes even over her mother, protecting them. Regina paused at the door and looked at Irisa in the half-light reflected from the hallway. With her long blond hair falling over her round, soft, still-babyish face, she looked even lovelier than usual. "Sweetheart," Regina whispered, bending over the bed. "Mommy and Daddy are going to the hospital now. Meta will be sleeping in our bed if any of the kids need her." Irisa's eyes opened wide.

"Wait, Mommy," she said, reaching under the pillow for a note she had written. Regina opened the crumpled paper. "Dear Mommy, we love you and the new baby. Come home safe."

"Mommy loves you too, honey," Regina murmured, suddenly afraid to leave. Change for her had always signaled loss, and loss was the hardest thing to bear. "I'll take this with me to the hospital for good luck," she said.

"Hey now, what's going on in here?" Ernest drawled, leaning against Irisa's door. "I thought we were in such a big hurry. I've already got your bag in the car and the engine's running."

Regina stood up and walked reluctantly toward him. Instinctively she stood as close to him as possible. He took her arm and guided her out of the house and around to the passenger side of the 1974 white Plymouth station wagon. She needed the sense of his presence, the feeling of his broad, six-foot-one-inch frame protecting her.

As they pulled away from the curb, Regina glanced back at Nasturtium Street, a quaint block right off the traffic circle in the town of Sebring, Florida. The roomy two-story house with the screened-in front porch had children asleep in each bedroom. To some people it would have seemed like a modest, working-class home, but to Regina it was like something out of a fairy tale. All the dreams of her life were safely enclosed inside.

A sharp contraction interrupted her thoughts, bringing her back to the reality of the moment. "Oh hurry, honey," she moaned. "The pains are getting worse."

Keeping one hand on the wheel and driving slightly faster than usual, Ernest reached for her hand. "Now, dear," he said. "Just do your breathing. You know we can't be going through red lights and stop signs."

She held his hand tightly, slowly releasing pressure on it as the pain subsided. Then she rested her head on his shoulder. The red-and-black flannel shirt softened the hardness of his body.

Regina closed her eyes. She knew from past experience that

she might as well rest while she could. She turned Ernest's hand over in hers. Then she lifted it from her lap onto her hard, contracting belly and kept it there. "Oh, Ernest, feel the baby, feel it. I wish I could keep it a little bit longer."

Regina loved the movement of life within her. It almost filled the emptiness and the relentless longing of her childhood. She could never love her children too much because she was not only giving them what she knew they needed, she was also making up for the love she never received enough of as a young child, the breasts, the arms, the warmth, the nurturing of a mother in that magical time before words.

When they finally pulled into the large, nearly empty parking lot at Hardee Memorial Hospital, they paused just long enough to notice the full moon shining over the orange groves and trailer park directly across from the modern, two-story, beige hospital.

Ernest put his arm around Regina's shoulder and led her through the front door into the lobby. After getting instructions from a receptionist, they pushed open a set of double doors and walked past a bronze plaque listing H. L. Coker as a board member of the hospital and a commemorative plaque for Bryant Coker.

On another night they might also have been greeted by Velma Coker, who had often done volunteer work in the hospital. Just three days before Regina arrived, after almost ten years of trying to become pregnant, Velma's daughter, Barbara Coker Mays, had finally given birth. The baby, delivered by emergency caesarean section, would, as events unfolded, turn out to have a congenitally malformed heart. The doctors feared the baby might die at any time.

Once inside the hospital labor room, Regina looked nervously at Dr. Black. "Oh, please don't make me go through this without anything," she begged. "I'm such a coward."

"We'll take it one step at a time," he answered. "I'll give

8

you some Demerol now and a saddle block, if you need it, when you're fully dilated." Then he turned to Ernest. "Adding another Twigg to the family tree? When is she putting you out to pasture?" Ernest shrugged, embarrassed, and dropped his eyes. Regina, who was between contractions, managed to flash one of those radiant smiles that made her look like an eighteen-year-old girl again.

The six-foot-tall, slender doctor, with a touch of gray in his hair, smiled back. Celia Warrington was right: Dr. Black had a good rapport with his patients. In his own easygoing way he made Regina feel that he cared about her and Ernest and their baby.

Dena Spieth, an experienced, middle-aged registered nurse, was also on duty that evening. She checked Regina's contractions, monitored the baby's fetal heart sounds and administered the medication. Labor moved quickly. At about three o'clock in the morning, when Regina was fully dilated, Spieth wheeled her into the delivery room, draped her, put her in stirrups and prepared her for the saddle block.

The next thing Regina remembered was the proud glow on Ernest's face and the euphoria she felt when she was told that the baby was a girl.

"Congratulations," Dr. Black said, grinning, still holding the baby upside down by her feet. "Looks like you have a healthy little girl." The baby was handed to the nurse, who put silver nitrate drops in her eyes, washed her and gave her Aquamephyton for blood clotting. The baby's Apgar score was checked by Dr. Black and recorded as a perfect ten.

When it was almost time for Regina to leave the delivery room, Spieth opened the cabinet and removed three bands with printed identification numbers from a roll. Then she took three blank strips of paper and wrote Regina's name, hospital number, the date, Dr. Black's name and the time of delivery on each of them.

She put the strips into the Ident-a-bands and attached one

to Regina's wrist, one to the baby's wrist and one to the baby's ankle. Before cutting each band to the right length, Spieth put her finger in the space between the skin and the band to be sure that the band would not be too tight or too loose. After that she clamped the band down using the pressure of her index finger and thumb.

The system had been developed so that the bands could not fall off or be unclasped in any way. Once a clasp had been opened, the band was ruined. They were designed to be cut off on discharge. It was one of several safeguards used by Hardee Memorial Hospital to be sure that babies could not accidentally be switched.

At about five o'clock that morning, the baby was placed in Regina's arms as she lay on the gurney, and the two were wheeled upstairs together. Regina closed her eyes. She felt her tiny daughter lying against her. Suddenly she was very tired. With the baby's heart beating against hers, she rested until it was time to nurse. She had never produced a lot of milk but had always started her children out on the breast so they could get the colostrum and what she believed was the best start she could give them.

Toward evening Regina's spirits were high. Her energy was renewed. She felt excited and eager for someone to talk to. The woman sharing her room was Mexican and spoke no English. Dr. Black said that walking was good for her, so at about six o'clock, Regina put on her robe and slippers and began to walk down the hall toward the nursery. She moved slowly and carefully because she had a tendency to hemorrhage after her deliveries.

As she approached room 210B, a private room, she saw a tall, slender young woman holding a baby dressed only in a diaper and undershirt. The baby's blanket had been taken off, and it looked to Regina as if the mother had just finished diapering or studying her new baby. Regina stopped in front of the open door and leaned against the door frame to rest. The mother's eyes met hers. She had a sharp, pretty face.

"Hi. What did you have?" Regina asked, smiling.

"A girl," the woman answered. But there was no joy in her expression. She clutched the baby against her and looked down.

Just then, a floor nurse walked down the corridor carrying a bedpan. When she saw the interaction, she put her arm around Regina and quickly guided her away. "That's a very sad situation," she whispered, as if she were about to share a confidence. Regina, who was naturally curious, waited for more. She felt uncomfortable about asking any questions because she had been taught long ago, as a child living in the orphanage, that she had no right to pry into other people's business.

But the nurse hurried away without giving an explanation of the sad situation. Regina shrugged and returned to her room. Her own exuberance had been temporarily muted by the experience. It was one of the things that didn't mean much then but that she remembered only many years later, when everything about the delivery and hospital stay meant a great deal.

The next morning at about ten o'clock, a nurse wheeled a baby into her room and handed it to her. Regina took the baby and automatically put it against her breast. The child lay limp in her arms. She looked down at it and frowned. Then she looked back up at the nurse and said, "This doesn't look like the same baby."

"It doesn't look like the same baby?" the nurse echoed, sounding astonished. "What do you mean it doesn't look like the same baby? Don't be silly. What's wrong with you? Why wouldn't it be the same baby?"

"My baby has strawberry blond hair and pink skin. This one has brownish-blond hair and a dusky complexion."

"Every mother says that. You're just a nervous mother. That's your name on the armband, isn't it?"

Regina lifted the tiny hand and saw the identification bracelet that said "Twigg." Even before she nodded in confused agreement, the nurse said, "Now check her ankle bracelet. See, like I told you, you're just a nervous mother."

As the nurse hurried out, Regina tried again to turn the baby's face to her breast. The infant seemed ill and had trouble nursing. Regina lifted her up, thinking that maybe she needed to burp. She looked at her again very closely. The baby's skin definitely looked darker than Regina had remembered. Now she noticed that there was also a blueness around her lips. "Oh my God, she's turning blue," Regina said out loud. "I must be trying too hard to make her suck.

"Excuse me, but I can't get her to eat," Regina called, as the nurse walked past. "I don't know why. She did fine yesterday, but now she's turning blue."

"Oh, don't worry about it," the nurse said, coming into the room and taking the baby away from Regina. "I'll give her some sugar water when I bring her back to the nursery."

When Ernest arrived at six-fifteen that evening, Regina's fears poured out in a rush to him. She sounded strange and wild. "Ernest, I know you're going to think I'm crazy, but the baby they brought me today doesn't look like our baby. She's darker. The first time they brought her I thought it was just me, but tonight I noticed it again."

Ernest looked at her as if she were totally out of her mind. "Don't talk like that, Regina," he said impatiently. "That's really sick. It's crazy. I don't ever want to hear you talk like that again, understand?" Regina could see the anger rising in him. "What's wrong with you?" he snapped.

The old insecurity seized her. Ernest was so happy and I'm spoiling everything, she thought. She became quiet, shadowy, submissive. "I guess I'm wrong. I must be crazy or just too nervous. I'm sorry, honey," she said. "Maybe she just picked up the darker look because of the Indian blood in your family and it took a while to show up."

"Probably," Ernest said. He had always been proud of his distant American Indian ancestry. He was sorry he had been so harsh with her. "Get some rest, sweetheart. I think you're just tired. I'll be back to get you in the morning. And remember," he added, the troubled look returning, "the kids are all excited, so you better calm down and get that crazy idea out of your head."

At ten o'clock right after Ernest arrived to pick Regina up, Dr. Palmer, a slender man in his late forties with a full head of gray hair, came into the room. A nurse was standing beside him.

Dr. Palmer was well known in the area, both as a physician and as a prominent member of the community. Regina stiffened when she saw the expression on his face. She knew instantly that something was wrong. As a creature long familiar with bad news, she could almost smell it the way an animal smells fear or danger.

Regina's eyes darted past the nurse to see if the baby's bassinet was in the hall. She was used to the nurse bringing the baby, and if something was wrong and Dr. Palmer was there then surely the baby must have something to do with it. "Dr. Sedaros is out of town today," Palmer began. His voice was bland. "I'll be taking over as your pediatrician."

"Where's the baby?" Regina asked nervously.

"We need to talk to you for a few minutes before we bring her in," he answered, pulling up a chair and putting it next to Ernest's. "Mrs. Twigg." He cleared his throat. "We understand from your chart that there is a history of heart disease in your family. And that you had a little girl who died of a heart problem."

Regina had been sitting up at attention; now suddenly she wished she could lie down. She wanted to pull her knees up to her chest and pull the covers over her head to make the bad things disappear, as she had when she was a child in the orphanage. But she didn't. She drew in her breath and held Ernest's hand tighter to control the trembling that had begun in her own.

"I'm sorry to have to tell you, but this baby has a very serious congenital heart condition too."

It took the doctor less than a minute to say it, but what did time matter? Time had stopped or moved backward. All Regina could think of was her last baby girl, Vivia, warm, alive, and beautiful one minute, blue and dead in her arms the next.

It was August 23, 1975.

They were a thousand miles from home on a four-lane highway heading out of Jellico, Tennessee, going to visit Ernest's mother, who was being treated for uterine cancer. All four little girls were with them.

After Vivia's delivery, they had been told that Vivia had a heart problem. Tetralogy of Fallot, the doctor called it. He said that at three months she should be taken to a large cardiac hospital for evaluation. But without warning, right there in the car, at just six weeks, she died.

"Ernest," Regina said, "the baby's not breathing right."

"She's just under stress," he answered. "Don't worry, we'll be there soon." A minute later Vivia was frantically gasping for breath. Her eyes rolled to the top of her head; she turned purple. Regina felt her stiffen.

"Oh my God," Regina screamed. "She can't breathe. Ernest, she can't breathe."

Panicked, Ernest pulled over, laid the baby on the seat and began administering cardiopulmonary resuscitation. Regina jumped out of the car and into the road, waving both arms in the air in a desperate attempt to stop a passing car, hoping that somehow the people inside it would be able to do what she and Ernest could not.

A woman in the passenger seat turned to stare as the car whizzed past. Regina's head was thrown back, her mouth was open, her arms were flailing. When the car didn't stop, Regina jumped into the driver's seat and began tearing down the highway toward the hospital. As they passed the car, the woman turned her head again. This time she waved.

Regina's car careened violently, and the three other little girls sitting in the backseat began to cry. As they arrived at the hospital, the car skidded and landed in a ditch. Ernest grabbed the baby and ran wildly toward the emergency room. It was too late. Vivia was pronounced dead on arrival at the tiny hospital in Jellico, Tennessee.

For the next three months, Regina hung on by a thread. She was hurt so badly by the loss that Ernest thought she would never recover. Night after night she'd wake up from a troubled sleep at four o'clock in the morning, dreaming of Vivia dying in her arms. Every night when Regina closed her eyes, that baby died again. When she opened her eyes, the night stretched out before her, full of danger and uncertainty. Even morning with its light left her lost in a world of internal darkness. One morning Ernest reached for her and pressed his face against hers. She could feel his breathing and the stubble of his beard against her skin.

"I'd better be getting the kids ready for school. I don't want them to be late," she said, moving away, without looking to see what time it was, without caring. Another dead, monotonous day. What did it matter?

"The only person who can keep you from losing it all is yourself," he said, withdrawing, and getting out on his side of the bed. He was hurt because he knew that for the first time she was unable to turn to him.

"But Ernest," she said, "how do I stop grieving? I carried

that baby inside me for nine months, I gave her life by the power of Almighty God, and six weeks later I watched her die."

"You've got the other babies to think of now, Regina. They need you."

"I know, I know," she answered mechanically. She wanted to listen to Ernest, but she couldn't. It wasn't until weeks later, when she heard a scream in the hallway and ran out to find Normia chasing Gina with a toy frog that anything seemed real. Somehow that strange, funny incident brought her back for a moment. And in that moment she saw the other children again and understood that they needed her.

That was three years ago. Now as she sat on the bed at Hardee Memorial Hospital it was all coming back. Dr. Palmer was saying something about taking the baby to the University of Miami Hospital. Ernest was nodding calmly and agreeing. Suddenly Regina was crying as if a dam had burst, sobbing, with tears pouring down her face, and at the same time still telling herself that this was just another nightmare and wondering why it was lasting so long. She knew it couldn't be a dream; still, it seemed unreal. She struggled to absorb the moment, to hear something hopeful. She needed hope to keep the other memory from coming back again. She was trying to watch the doctor and nurse for a smile or a word or a sign of reassurance.

The nurse was talking quickly, saying something about bringing the papers to them to sign for discharge, and Dr. Palmer was telling Ernest that he'd like to see the baby in his office before they took her home.

The nurse left the room, and when she returned she had the baby in the bassinet and the papers in her hand. She kept bouncing back and forth from the baby to the papers, her dark shadow dancing on the wall.

Finally she stood still. She said it was time to check the identification number on Regina's band with the number on the baby's. Through the foggy haze of grief, Regina heard her reading from a piece of paper. Her voice sounded faraway. " 'I certify that during the discharge procedure I received my baby, examined it, and determined it was mine. I checked the Ident-a-band parts sealed on the baby and on me and found that they were identically numbered 1059 and contained correct identifying information.'

"Now Mrs. Twigg," the nurse said sharply, "read those numbers back to me. Mrs. Twigg," she repeated, "I need your attention. This is part of our discharge procedure. I'd like you to receive the baby now. Please examine it and determine that it is yours. After you've done that, I will cut the band off her wrist and tape it onto the record right here in front of you, as you watch. That's our protocol." Finally she paused. Regina nodded blankly and repeated the numbers in a daze. "Sign here. Good. Now that's a good girl," the nurse said.

The nurse put the baby down on the bed and began unfolding and refolding the receiving blanket. Regina couldn't see exactly what the nurse was doing because she was drying her eyes and face with a handful of tissues and trying to regain her composure. What she did remember many years later was the flat, emotionless, matter-of-fact way that the nurse said, "Here," as she stood at arm's length and held the baby with the blue lips and dusky skin out to her.

A few minutes later Ernest and Regina Twigg left Hardee Memorial Hospital carrying Barbara Coker Mays's sick baby. Nine years would pass before they discovered that she was not their daughter.

The Voice of
Regina Twigg

All my life, as far back as I can remember, I longed for a family that was really mine. My strongest memory of childhood, after my mother was taken from us, was of the family I lost. I would look out the window at the endless two-lane highway in front of the children's home in Wellsville, Ohio, and at the Ohio River with the paddle wheel barges that ran beside it, and dream of my beautiful mother laughing and singing songs with all the children gathered around her.

I had entered the home at the age of three. All of the youngest children lived upstairs, the little girls on one side and the little boys on the other side. They kept the boys and girls separate so I never really got to see my brother. Sometimes we would see each other for a second out on the playground if we were lucky and if they took both sets of kids out at the same time. But that was all. If I got a glimpse of him I was allowed to say, "Hi, Joey," and that was about it.

I will always remember my twin sisters with their beautiful strawberry blond hair glistening in the sunshine. When somebody took me away to adopt me, all I could do was cry and cry and cry to be with my sisters again. Finally, the people decided I couldn't adjust, so they sent me back to the orphanage. But when I got back, my twin sisters were gone. When I realized they had been adopted, I started to cry and sob. A lady who worked at the orphanage told me to shut up. "Oh, shut up," I can remember her saying. "Just shut up."

In all, I was taken for trial adoptions three different times. The third time I stayed with the people. The sad part is that the first people were really nice people and they really loved me. The woman gave me a doll when she sent me back, and I have it to this day. They lived in Leetonia, Ohio. I don't know if they're still alive or not. They had a boy named Richard. I begged them to please take my sisters home too. But they didn't want to do that; they only wanted one child.

Years later I learned that like me my sisters never felt loved; they didn't believe that they were really wanted or fit in. They had always been happy, bubbly little girls, just as normal as any other kids. But now, even though they had been placed in adoptive homes, they felt rejected. These feelings ran very deep. I believe that if the orphanage hadn't been torn down, if we all had stayed there, we would not have had such deep scars or suffered a lot of the pain that we did. At the children's home, lonely as it was, we had a sense of unity with the other children. We all banded together, and in a way we almost formed our own parentless families. I'm not saying there wasn't squabbling. Naturally there were differences, but it was as if the children were together against the world. And since the world was very, very scary without anybody there for you, the children clung together and supported each other.

So it was the children against the world; it was the children banding together, almost entirely isolated from the rest of the world. At the age of nine, I still had never tasted eggs or bacon. I had only eaten grits and gruel. I had never seen a telephone or a newspaper, and I had very little understanding of what it meant to be part of a real family.

I was in my second trial adoptive home for only one week. I had gone from the first home back to the children's home, and then this family in New Amsterdam, Ohio, took me. I had not been fed properly as a baby because my mother didn't have money to buy enough food for us, so I had extremely bowed legs. When this lady took me home and saw my bowed legs, she screamed, "Oh my God! I didn't know she was so bowlegged. I'll send her back."

I was there for one week and I just kissed the ground she walked on because by this time I knew that my older sisters were gone, and I wouldn't have them anymore. My baby sister had already been taken, and I never saw my brother again either. I had lived in the orphanage for five years, and at age eight I wanted desperately to stay with these people and have a home, but she sent me back because of my bowed legs.

In those days people could pretty much come off the street and say, "I want some children, especially older children who just weren't adopted out." Basically, older children were considered unadoptable. I don't know how they managed to find homes for us. I remember being told, "Well, you're really at an unadoptable age, but we're tearing the children's home down, so we need to find someplace for you to go." I know that they were eagerly giving us to whoever called and inquired.

I felt like this whole big frightening world was out there. When I traveled from the children's home to the family court to a new trial home, I would look out the window at the expanse of green land and earth and the Catawall Barges. Then when I got back to the orphanage, I'd sit at my window for hours at a time singing the song "Far Away Places" and thinking of my mother.

My mother was gone. She was in a faraway place, and to this day I can't hear that song without crying over and over. I kept longing for my lost mother. Somehow I came to believe that she had died by jumping off a bridge.

Our orphanage was considered one of the better ones. At Christmastime, people from all over the town would send Christmas presents to the poor children. Some people would get a specific child to visit and maybe they'd send a gift or something during the year.

Mostly they had young high school girls supervising the small children. Some of these high school girls had severe emotional problems and would take their anger out on us. I still remember the children getting their little behinds beaten red for supposedly saying a bad word when they never actually did. The high school girls would beat them. My little sister Sophie got her behind beaten raw one day, absolutely fiery red. She screamed and screamed and screamed, but that girl just wouldn't stop beating her.

I don't remember seeing adults there very often. I know that there was a woman who was supposed to be in charge of the little girls, but she stayed in her room all the time. She practically never came out. It was the high schoolers who were actually in charge of us. Oh, we had a teacher in the little school, but she was just someone who came and left. She didn't stay right there. The man and woman who actually ran the children's home were downstairs in an office. They had their own suite downstairs but we never saw them either, almost never.

The sleeping arrangements were dormitory style, and some of the older children also had emotional problems. One girl tried to molest some of the small children. I remember the kids telling me that if she ever touched me or said anything to me, like asking me to get into bed with her, I should just start screaming. And so, when she finally did, I just started yelling my head off. She didn't get very far. I screamed like I was being beaten up, like I was getting a terrible spanking, that kind of scream. She jumped out of bed and all the children rushed to my rescue. That was the kind of bond that we all shared, an unspoken commitment to protect each other.

But the main bond I had was with my sisters and the brother that I rarely saw. I can still remember how we stood on the playground one day. It was near the time when they were just starting to get rid of the children, and we vowed, we absolutely swore, my twin sisters and my baby brother and my little sister, that we would never let anybody separate us, little knowing that there was nothing we could do about it.

Even today I still think back to little Sophie, whom I never found. She looked like Shirley Temple. People would ask her, "What's your name, little girl?" And she would stomp one foot and her little curls would bounce, and she would say, "My name is Sophie Joanne Gibbons."

I have often wondered if she still remembers that. If she knows who she is. The people who adopted her took her away in their car and drove off with her in front of my eyes. She was the youngest and the first to go. I don't recall her age. But I have a notion that she was adopted by someone—this is just a hunch—in Yorkville, Ohio.

I often wonder if she has any memories of us. Even though they would have changed her last name, probably her whole name, I wonder if she would still remember (that is, if she is alive) how she used to stomp her little foot and say her name, or if they changed her so that she doesn't want to remember. I wish I could find out what happened to her. I wish I could see her again. I hope that she would want to know me.

Years ago in Steubenville, Ohio, a lady came into a clothing store where I was working. She said, "You look like a girl, a young girl that I know in Yorkville, Ohio. You're her spitting image; you could be her sister. Do you have any relatives in Yorkville?"

"Oh, God, yes," I said, and I told her about the little sister I wanted to find who was taken away from me.

She instantly shut her mouth, said, "I have to leave," cutting the conversation off like it was poison, and hurried away. I tried to stop her and get her name, but I couldn't. I guess she was scared about giving information and causing trouble with the family if the girl really was my sister.

When they were first beginning to adopt the children out we didn't know why. We only found out later that they were tearing the home down.

On one particular day the kids started calling to me, "Someone's taking Sophie." I looked up and saw them walking away with her. I began to cry and scream. I wanted to run after her but someone held me.

The lady was wearing a two-piece green suit and the man's suit was brown. They were beautifully dressed and they had a fancy new car. A beautiful, brand-new car. And they got into the car with her and drove away. I didn't know what kind of car it was. I was too little to know. All I knew was that they were down near the road getting into the car and that they had my baby sister and that the road was off-limits.

It was another huge loss. My mother was my first loss and then Sophie. I can remember thinking to myself, "Sophie's gone, Sophie's gone, Sophie's gone. I'll never see her again."

In the years that followed, I remembered over and over how Sophie and I used to pick dandelions on the children's playground and tie them together to make necklaces out of them and wear them. We thought they were the prettiest things.

We also used to find rusty bobby pins along the driveway and put pin curls in our hair. We'd get yelled at because we weren't supposed to curl our hair.

We had no adults helping us grow up with any sense that we were lovable. All we had was discipline if they thought we had been lying or if we got on their nerves.

They had these swinging doors in the hallway that were painted with army-green paint. They would sit us behind these doors and make us stay there for hours. Sometimes we would sit there from morning to night. As we sat, we would scratch pictures in the paint. Pictures of houses, trees and flowers and stick figures of mothers, fathers and children. It wasn't really graffiti; they were just pictures of families and houses and pets and mothers and fathers. All the things we longed for and dreamt about but didn't have.

When I was about eight, I broke both my arms when my sweaty hands caused me to fall from the maypole that I was climbing. I still remember that there was a girl in the hospital bed next to mine whose parents came to visit her every day. I thought she was so lucky to have a mommy and a daddy. No one came to visit me. I'll never forget the terrible sense of loneliness, of not being part of a real family. It stayed with me all the rest of my life.

After the second family rejected me, I was taken for a third trial adoption. I remember looking out the car window and watching the scenery go by, thinking, "What's going to happen to me now?"

Finally the car stopped. I was dropped off in Ohio on the border of two counties, Jefferson and Mahoning. My adoptive parents were waiting. My new mother was a large, buxom woman with a stern, unsmiling face. Her husband seemed quiet and distant. Apparently it was easier just to meet them there rather than have them come to the orphanage. I had never seen them before, but I just went from one car to the other. They had a six-month trial period to decide if they wanted me. There were four other adoptive children at home, three boys and a girl.

As it turned out, that was the home where I was to stay. They kept me, but in all those years, my adoptive mother never told me what I needed to hear more than anything else in the world: that she truly loved me. She just wasn't able to say that. She wasn't that kind of person.

Long after I was adopted I was still searching for a connection. At night I kept dreaming that I was back in the orphanage. In my dream the ceilings were high, the hallways were like a maze, and the structure was leaning in on itself and falling apart. I would call out to see if somebody was there, but no one would answer. For many years, even after I married Ernest and finally had someone of my own to love, the dream would come back in times of stress. In it I'd feel totally alone and hopelessly lost in the cobwebs and dirt. I had that dream over and over again after Vivia died.

Vivia's death reawakened all of my old childhood fears about the loss of my brother and sisters. On one level I believed her death was a single chance event. But on some other level there was always a dark feeling that I would lose another baby. I didn't know how, and then they told me about Arlena.

Chapter 2

Arlena's Childhood

Regina stood holding the baby in front of the house, her eyes red from crying. Ernest fumbled in his pocket for the keys. Before he could unlock the door, Irisa threw it open. Her face was flushed with excitement. She had swept the kitchen, vacuumed the living room and dusted everything she could reach. Now she stood waiting for Mommy and the baby with a bouquet of wildflowers the children had picked themselves.

"Oh, honey," Regina said, with big tears spilling out all over again at the sight of Irisa. "Our baby is sick."

Irisa frowned, but then her face relaxed. "You can fix her, Mommy."

Regina knew that the intensity of her love offered no protection against a damaged heart and frail body. She also knew she'd never convince Irisa. In a way it mirrored the irony of her early life.

She had always had the appearance of the strong and powerful, the fortunate, the golden-haired girl with the deep green eyes and the beautiful cheekbones. But her beauty only masked the malnutrition, poverty, submission and helplessness that she felt.

Irisa clung to her mother. "God will help you fix her, Mommy," she said. Regina stiffened. Irisa had watched Vivia die. Another death would be too much for the child; she could not allow it to happen.

She took Irisa's hand, picked up the baby and walked across the living room. "Yes, Mommy and Daddy will fix the baby," she murmured.

The University of Miami Hospital's Neonatal Intensive Care Cardiac Unit was filled with little bassinets holding pretty day-old babies hooked up to wires and tubes, infants like Arlena, still too young to cry when someone was about to stick them with a needle, too young to wonder if they would live until their next feeding. The parents often slept in visitors chairs for five or six days at a time just so they could be there if their babies needed them in the night. Since Regina could not travel so soon after the delivery, she had stayed at home with the children. Ernest had taken Arlena to Miami by himself.

During the catheterization, they injected red dye into Arlena's heart and visualized it on a screen. Dr. Delores Tamer, the pediatric cardiologist, was trying to see the inner workings. She was concerned and solicitous. She told Ernest that Arlena had only one working valve; three of the usual four valves to the heart were missing. Arlena also had no bottom ventricle and the major vessels were transposed. Dr. Tamer explained that she had to open up the upper chamber wall to allow the oxygenated blue and red blood to travel through Arlena's body. Without that procedure, she said, Arlena would not survive the week.

At the age of three, perhaps Arlena would be strong

enough for open-heart surgery, but for now surgery was out of the question. "It would kill her," said Dr. Tamer. "We will try to sustain her on digoxin. She has to have it morning, noon and night. Don't ever forget to give it to her. It's your only hope. How you regulate her medicine will determine whether she lives or dies."

At six weeks Arlena had pneumonia. After she recovered from that she kept getting croup. Finally she grew out of the croup. Anything that could cause an infection, like the flu, chickenpox or even a sore or a dental cavity, could kill her.

Still, the doctors told Ernest and Regina that Arlena was an amazing baby. They couldn't believe how well she tolerated the situation. At eight months she had to go back for a second catheterization. For nine hours she didn't move. Then suddenly she was awake and crying for milk.

Every six months they had to travel four hours each way to Miami for blood tests to check for iron in her system and for x-rays to see if her heart had become enlarged. When she was two years old, the doctors bent her neck back so far that Regina thought it would snap. They were checking for a pulse in one of the veins but could never seem to find it.

Even on her best days, you could feel her little heart beating through her back with your hand. It was a loud, powerful, laboring, machinelike sound. Despite it all, she was a remarkably beautiful and angelic baby with a sweetness and love of life that drew everyone toward her.

Chapter 3
Kimberly's Childhood

A tall, thin woman sat in a wheelchair, with braces on both her legs. Her sharp, pretty face was pale from chemotherapy and twisted with pain. A beautiful, blond toddler with large, green eyes that were surprisingly intense for a child so young bounced at her side. Behind them stood a slender man, blond like the child and the wig the woman wore. He was pushing the wheelchair.

"She's so young," Cindy thought as she stood up to greet them. Usually the terminal cancer patients that came to Tampa General Hospital for radiation treatment were old. At least the ones who had already been through surgery and chemotherapy. The ones that were close to dying. This woman looked about thirty, and her husband didn't look much older.

The little girl was laughing and jumping up and down, holding on to the arm of the wheelchair. She was so cute and so rambunctious and her mother was too sick to hold her. "What's going to happen to that poor baby when her mother dies?" Cindy thought while drawing her lips back into a smile and holding out her hand.

"I'm Cynthia Tanner," she said. Robert Mays handed her the completed financial forms. She looked at them. "Mr. Mays, are you the patient?" she asked, taking him in for the first time.

He flashed a quick condescending, bemused smile and met her eyes. "No," he answered, "it's my wife, Barbara."

"Sir," she said, "you answered all the questions on this form as if you were the patient." He shifted uncomfortably. "We need to know your wife's full name, date of birth, social security number and insurance, not yours."

Barbara smiled. She thought it was funny. "Bob likes to be at the center of things," she said.

"I'm sorry, sir, but you'll have to go back to the registration desk and correct this." Now the man looked annoyed. Barbara giggled. "I can keep the x-rays and the medical records and the little girl here, while you run back," Cindy offered.

"Thank you, but we can manage," Barbara said. Then as if she thought she might seem rude, she added, "I like to spend as much time with her as I can."

"I understand," Cindy said, embarrassed to realize that the woman knew how close she was to dying.

They came every day after that. The mother, the father and the little girl. The child was a real live wire, running around in the reception area, getting into the drawers and playing with an old broken intercom, while her mother was given radiation treatments. She was such a happy, pretty child that all of the nurses and therapists, receptionists and aides always ended up hugging her, playing with her and trying to amuse her. After all, they said, it was hard for a baby to sit still in a chair for an hour or two. Underneath, everyone felt sorry for her. It was a shame that she would soon be a motherless child.

Cindy just couldn't let go of the idea. Usually she was tough, reserved and efficient. But Kimberly was just a couple of years younger than her own daughter, Ashlee. She tried to imagine what would happen if she got cancer of the ovaries and died. What would happen to Ashlee? She couldn't even begin to deal with the thought. All they had was each other.

Cindy was the oldest of three children. Her father owned a garbage disposal service in Hillsborough County, Florida, and another in Pasco County. He made a good living. Her mother was a nurse. Cindy was used to nice clothes, nice cars and nice homes, but she had never been spoiled. She had been taught to save. It was a comfortable, middle-class childhood until her parents started having problems. Cindy couldn't handle the fighting so she ran away from home. She came back a few days later. Things were better for a while, but when she was seventeen her parents divorced. Cindy never got over it. A few years later they remarried, then divorced again in February of 1977.

For a while, after her own divorce, Cindy lived with her mother. She'd only been married for two months before everything fell apart. She knew she'd made a terrible mistake and she moved out, but she couldn't quite give him up. She saw him a couple of times and got pregnant.

Cindy and Ashlee had been living alone in a run-down trailer on the edge of town for as long as Ashlee could remember. Cindy worked three jobs to support them and to keep Ashlee in a good day care center. It wasn't exactly her dream of the perfect American family, but she handled it. Forty hours a week as a receptionist at Tampa General Hospital, Friday and Saturday nights as a cocktail waitress in a local bar and restaurant and Sunday as a typist in the radiation, oncology department at Tampa General.

It was nothing compared to what Barbara Coker Mays had to deal with. Part of Cindy's job was to do a daily census of the patients, so she always knew when Barbara was admitted for chemotherapy along with the radiation. Cindy would try to get over and see her. They all would, the therapists and the nurses and the aides. Mostly it was small talk. But the one day that Cindy couldn't get out of her mind, Barbara had looked up, with that pale, pretty face and said, "Do you know what I want more than anything else in the world?"

"No," Cindy said, thinking maybe she could get it for her.

"To be alive on Kimberly's second birthday."

Sometimes Cindy would run into Barbara's mother, Velma Coker, in the lobby. A couple of times she tried to strike up a conversation but Mrs. Coker didn't seem interested. Cindy tried not to think she was a snob.

Maybe Barbara was going to have another chemotherapy treatment or another operation, she reasoned. Who knows how people react under those kinds of circumstances? Barbara was the one who mattered, and Barbara wanted to talk.

Once when Cindy visited her, Mrs. Coker was there. Barbara was always kind and gentle and sweet. She tried to introduce Cindy to her mother and to have them make friends. Cindy was on one side of the bed and Mrs. Coker was on the other. Mrs. Coker kept acting as if Cindy weren't even standing there. Cindy remained determined not to let it bother her.

She was seeing a lot of Barbara and Bob, and she knew there was tension between them. She thought Mrs. Coker had something to do with it. What a shame, she thought, to be fighting with so little time left. You'd think that if people were dying, they'd treasure every last moment and keep saying thank you and I love you, so they'd be remembered that way. But that just wasn't how it worked.

The last time she walked into Barbara's room unannounced, she knew right away that she shouldn't have come. Bob was leaning over the bed, holding Barbara's hand. He seemed upset. She pulled her hand away and started crying. She looked lost and bewildered. Cindy tried to back out, hoping to leave quietly before they saw her. There was a little vase with a couple of roses in it that a minister had brought to Barbara earlier in the afternoon. Cindy backed right into it and knocked it onto the ground.

"Oh, Barbara, I'm so sorry," she said. "I'll replace it." Her voice was husky. And for just a moment when Bob caught her eye, she thought she saw something different in his expression.

"You know, Bob," she said the next time they met. "It's normal for cancer patients to regress and to want to be with their mothers again. Some go back almost to birth. I've seen patients come into this department in wheelchairs in a fetal position. Unconsciously, Barbara might be hoping her mother can take care of her and make her better, like when she was a child."

Bob shrugged. "If she's my wife, I should be able to take care of her."

"Hey, I understand that, Bob," Cindy said, putting her hand on his arm. "But maybe she's trying to say goodbye to her mother and her baby."

He nodded as if he understood. "You're right, Cindy. She knows she's dying. She has a lot to come to terms with."

Chapter 4

The Phone Call

The phone rang in the old house on Nasturtium Street. "Hello," Regina said. There was a pause.

"Is this Mrs. Twigg?" a woman on the other end asked.

"Yes," Regina answered, scooping up Arlena and holding her on her lap as she spoke.

"You probably don't remember me, Mrs. Twigg," the woman said, "but I was in the hospital the same time you were. We both had baby girls. I know your baby was not well. I know she was very sick when she was born and I was just wondering how she's doing."

"Oh, wow," Regina gasped, dumbfounded. "That was almost two years ago. I can't believe you still remember and you're calling after such a long time."

"Well," the woman said, "I often wondered about her. I guess that's just the kind of person I am. I just care."

"Gosh," Regina responded, still amazed. "It's so nice of you to be reaching out to me. I can really use a friend. My baby's still very sick. She almost died. We've been taking her to Miami every six months for tests. She's the greatest little girl."

"Well," the woman continued, "I have a little blond-haired baby girl too, the same age and everything, and I was just thinking maybe we could get together sometime soon and the children could play."

"Sure, oh sure," Regina answered. "That would be really nice. I'd like to see your little girl."

"I'd like to see yours too," the woman said.

"How's Wednesday?" Regina asked. Suddenly the woman on the other end of the phone began to cry and cry. "Hey," Regina said, confused, "what's wrong? Are you all right?"

Then she heard another woman's voice in the background. "Honey, you need to get off the phone right now. You're not well."

"I'm sorry," the other woman said, taking the phone and talking to Regina. "She's sick. She'll have to call you back another time." The phone went dead.

Regina sat there for a few minutes, then she picked up the phone and called her friend Betty Parker. "Betty," she said, "I just got the strangest phone call."

"Boy, Regina," Betty responded, after hearing the story. "Nobody ever called me up after two years and talked to me and cared about my babies that way."

All morning Wednesday Regina waited. A white car pulled up at around noon. Regina and the kids were watching from the screened porch. She thought she saw three adults and a child looking toward the porch from inside the car. "They're here," Regina called to the kids. But as she walked toward the porch door, the car drove away.

Chapter 5
A New Romance

One Friday night, Cindy was taking Ashlee to the baby-sitter's house. She was right near Bob and Barbara's apartment, had a little extra time and decided to stop by. "Ashlee," she said, "there's someplace we're going to stop in Brandon. I've got some friends I want to say hello to for a minute."

Bob opened the door, and was surprised to see Cindy. His voice was soft and uncertain; his eyes were red and he looked worn. "She left me," he said. "I came home and she was gone. I offered to get a nurse to stay with her during the day but she said no. I went to a meeting over in Stanford one day, and when I came home the house was empty. No wife, no baby, no baby bed, no dishes. Her parents came. They took almost everything. They moved her to Wauchula."

"Oh, Bob," Cindy said. "I can't believe it. I'm so sorry. I just came by to say hello and introduce you to Ashlee. I had no idea." She stood there feeling awkward, groping for words.

There was an uncertain silence. He coughed. "Would you like to come in? Do you have time?"

"No, I really can't right now. I've got to get to work. But please, let me know if I can help," she said, holding her hand out to him, feeling his strong firm grip and avoiding his eyes. They opened up too many feelings. They disturbed and un-settled her.

For a while after that she lost track of Bob and Barbara. She didn't know what had happened. She thought about calling Barbara and asking if she could come and visit. But Cindy never really liked getting in the middle of other people's business. She thought about calling Bob, but somehow that made her uncomfortable too. She figured she had already gotten too involved. Now and then she wondered if they had ever gotten divorced, if Barbara had died or if they had got-ten back together.

One night, in mid February of 1981, Cindy was in the bar where she worked, though she wasn't working that night. She'd gone to a town festival with a friend, and they decided to stop on the way home to have a drink. They went to that bar because she knew everybody. The bartenders, the wait-resses and the regular customers, divorced and single women, blue-collar workers and a few professionals. All of them bored by the lives they lived, looking for relief from their aching shoulders and dull routines. A new rhythm, a little excitement, a body to hold on to, at least for a song in the hot, smoky darkness.

Cindy felt protected by that crowd, confident and comfort-able in it. She looked up and all of a sudden saw Bob sitting at a table with another man. Walking over and smiling, she held out her hand. "Bob," she said. "How have you been? What are you doing here?"

"This is Dave, my boss," he answered, smiling. "We were having a meeting, then went to dinner and decided to have a couple of drinks."

That was the night she heard about everything. How Barbara, a tall, beautiful blonde, had pinned a note to his car ten years earlier. "Hey hotshot," it said, "when are you gonna take me for a ride?"

Barbara got her ride and married Bob a year later. She worked as a beautician at Jewel's Beauty Shop; he worked at a citrus harvesting company owned by her family. She was the youngest of three children. He was the oldest of two. His mother had a second baby when he was eighteen. His father was a career air force man who moved around a lot. Bob had started school in Okinawa. When he finished high school he took a year off and traveled around Europe. The air force was looking for him when he came home. It was 1964 and the heart of the Vietnam War. They assigned him to a base in Germany. He flew in and out of Vietnam on temporary duty assignments and managed to take a few courses. He was never much of a student. He was bright, charming and good with language. Everyone liked him. Barbara was also charming and gracious. They seemed like a perfect couple. It was love at first sight.

They settled in Orlando and began trying to have a baby almost immediately. After nearly ten years of temperature taking and fertility experts, just when they were about to give up, Barbara became pregnant. The pregnancy went well, but Barbara didn't go into labor. Bob finally had to drive her to Hardee Memorial in his pickup truck so they could induce labor. Even that didn't work. In the end they had to perform a caesarean section because the fetal heart monitor registered severe fetal distress. Dr. William Black was the obstetrician, but they also called in Dr. Ernest Palmer and Dr. Adley Sedaros just to watch over everything.

It was a hard recovery for Barbara, but she was ecstatic. The first year and a half with Kimberly was her happiest time.

Then one morning Barbara woke up in agony. When Bob

took her to the hospital, the doctors discovered massive, widespread ovarian cancer. "Maybe six months," they told him. He decided to tell her himself.

"I already know," she said when she saw his face. "I'm not going to be able to have any more babies."

"Barbara," he said, "they found some cancer." Kimberly was just a toddler. That's when the radiation and the chemotherapy began. After that, Barbara had a colostomy because the radiation had burned a hole through her colon.

"I think she just didn't feel pretty anymore," Bob said. "And she didn't want me to see her that way."

Barbara filed for divorce a few months later, and Bob borrowed money from his parents for a retainer to hire an attorney. When they went to court they took all of her medical records and gave them to the judge. As they wheeled Barbara in, it was obvious she didn't have long to live. Bob had all this great medical coverage that Barbara would need if she were ever hospitalized again. He even had coverage for her medication, so the judge looked at this and just threw out her request for a divorce.

"It will be a legal separation," he ruled. "She will have custody of Kimberly for as long as she lives; he will have visitation every other weekend."

Bob had finished talking, and he drank his Jack Daniel's and put his face in his hands. In the candlelight, Cindy could see the fine, golden hair on his arms. His boss asked her to dance.

"You're all Bob ever thinks about," the boss said, moving easily but holding his arm stiff to keep a space between them. "You're all he talks about."

"What do you mean?" Cindy asked, amazed.

"Oh, he must have told you how grateful he is that you stopped by and visited. How good you are with Kimberly, how attractive you are, what a great person you are."

The music was still playing. Cindy was moving to it, Bob's boss was moving, but now there was a new sensation in her that had a powerful silent rhythm of its own. She looked up.

"He came here tonight just to find you. Just hoping you'd be here. Bob's very lonely, Cindy," the boss said. "Why don't you ask him to dance?"

When the song ended, she moved toward Bob, almost in a dream. He stood up and held out his arms. The song "Can I Have This Dance for the Rest of My Life" had started playing. She smiled, and he smiled back, that warm, familiar smile that made him look young and old at the same time. That easy, charming smile that she noticed the very first time they met.

"I'll take you home tonight," he whispered, putting his arms around her waist and pulling her close.

She was a stable, sensible woman with a strong, firm body and efficient movements. Even her short, blond, curly hair, blue eyes and warm laugh failed to make her look delicate. There was something practical, almost tough, about Cindy Tanner. She was down-to-earth and hardworking. She had tried love and marriage and it had failed. Her feelings were under her control. She had a life of her own and a trailer and Ashlee and three jobs. She felt some apprehension and some excitement. She felt his need and his power.

In the car, he took her hand. "Remember that day in the hospital when you knocked over the vase?" he said, laughing. "That was the first time I knew I had feelings for you."

She laughed too, a breathless laugh, feeling open and shy at the same time. He parked the car in the driveway and turned toward her, looking at her with a heavy, longing, intense look. She pulled back. He saw her fear and resistance and instantly changed his approach.

"Next weekend, when I have Kimberly," he said lightly, "I want to bring her over. We can all do something together." Already he knew that the child was a magnet between them, more powerful even than passion. A man like Bob, even a charming, handsome man with an easy smile and smooth manner, might be resistible to a woman like Cindy. But a tiny child, a beautiful, innocent baby, who would soon be mother-less—how could she say no to Kimberly?

"Yes," she said, "yes."

And the word caught in her throat as he leaned toward her, pressing his soft, open mouth against hers.

"Sweetheart," he breathed, and her heartbeat quickened, warning her away and at the same time drawing her toward him.

Chapter 6
The Twiggs

Arlena's illness took every extra dime. Ernest's insurance paid two thousand dollars for each catheterization, but Regina and Ernest still had five hundred left to pay. Of course, the medical bills wiped out anything they could have used for the other children. The kids had clothes to wear, they had food to eat, but they wore the same couple of pairs of blue jeans off and on for the whole school year. That's how hard it was. But they wore a clean pair every day; Regina made sure of that. When it came to groceries they often ran short. They couldn't buy the extras that other families had in their refrigerators. They had necessities and that was about it. One year they had scrambled eggs for Thanksgiving because they couldn't afford a turkey.

Arlena's health fluctuated back and forth. Sometimes she seemed to do so well that you would almost wonder if she was getting better. On her good days, people would look at her and think that there was practically nothing wrong with her. Of course, she still had a dusky complexion and a bluish tinge to her lips. Sometimes her energy level was high. At other times she would become really weak. Her eyes would take on the weary look of a child who had always lived with pain. A child who knew that some days her legs would not carry her.

Once when the children were all playing in the backyard Regina said, "Ernest, you need to make her quit. You need to make her stop." Ernest had brushed it off.

"Oh, let her play. Let her have some fun," he answered. She was going after her daddy with a ball and she ran and ran and ran. Regina could see she was getting more and more blue. Just as Regina was going to assert herself, pick Arlena up and force her to quit, Arlena passed out and fell down. Regina picked her up and carried her inside. After a few minutes the child revived and her heartbeat stabilized. But Regina was reminded all over again that normal exertion could push Arlena past her limit.

Just the same, she was remarkably active. She would put on a pair of roller skates and skate up and down the sidewalk. She learned how to ride a tricycle and then a bike. It wasn't easy for her, but she was always spirited. Once when her sister Gina was teaching her how to balance, she suddenly flew over the handlebars and landed on her bottom. At first she was frightened, but she just picked herself up when she realized she wasn't hurt, and laughed and laughed.

Every Sunday morning there was a church meeting. Except for when the children were sick, Regina was there with all of them, their faces scrubbed and shiny, lined up across one pew. On Sunday and on Wednesday nights they were back at the cream-colored, concrete-block nondenominational Church of Christ, singing songs and learning stories from the Bible. On other evenings, Regina would play with them, read to them and sing to them. Regina wrote down-home country songs and then sang them as she played the piano. The depth and power of her voice mirrored the passion and intensity of her life. If things had been different, she might have become another country-western star. From time to time, she performed the songs she had written. Once, while Arlena and the other children looked on adoringly, she sang a song she had written about the endangered manatee to three thousand people at the Blue Springs Manatee Festival.

The children dominated her days and her nights. They often appeared in her dreams. Years earlier in the orphanage she had lost her sense of identity, and with the children she had regained it. They were the proof that she had survived. She was clearly their mother, and when she was with them her face relaxed and became girlish. Her speech softened and slowed; her eyes glowed. She walked proudly, a mother who loved her children and was responsible for them.

Around other grown women, though, Regina was still unsure of herself. She longed for the acceptance of a friend, but she felt different, self-conscious, more plainly dressed than the others. Her head was filled with thoughts of Arlena becoming sick and dying. At social gatherings she braced herself. Sometimes when she felt the disapproval of the other women, her eyes narrowed and her face became pale and immobile. She lowered her head in an automatic posture of submission.

She knew these women thought she had too many children and that her house was too small and too crowded. Who did she think she was, Ethel Kennedy? Didn't she know she was just a poor woman with a cradle and an ironing board?

Evenings were the loneliest time, with the children asleep and Ernest at work. Part of Regina's routine was to pick up the toys that the children left scattered each day. Sometimes while putting the toys back into the big trunk that she had painted a bright and cheerful red, she felt inexplicably sad. As she sat beside the trunk, surrounded by the toys and the silence, she might even cry like a child herself, suddenly feeling unfinished, empty and very much alone.

Will, who was just ten months older than Arlena, was also sick. Born with walleye strabismus, he underwent serious eye surgery at eighteen months. So there were two cradles at the side of her bed and two sick babies in diapers crying out during the night. And Regina was pregnant again. More and more often work kept Ernest away.

Still, it was a happy marriage. As far as Regina was concerned, it would always be a happy marriage. She needed her husband and her children too badly to even consider that it was anything else.

There were some scars, painful issues settled and unsettled. There was a woman at work who began to call the house quite regularly asking Ernest for favors and help around her house. Regina had heard whispered rumors about the twice-divorced woman with the body that wouldn't quit. The phone calls and a change in Ernest's attitude at home troubled Regina enough to make her stop by unannounced one day with the children to take a look.

The very sight of that slender, braless woman parading around in front of Ernest, baiting him, infuriated Regina. She knew better than anyone that he was a man and could be tempted just like anyone else. "I take good care of Ernie," the woman had said, smiling.

"Oh," Regina replied, "I take good care of him too."

There were no confessions or recriminations and Regina refused to let one tramp destroy her family or poison her marriage. She was prepared to fight for Ernest if necessary and to keep him.

After that, she treated Ernest with more love, more responsiveness and more tenderness than ever before. He told her that he was faithful and she accepted it. But sometimes, especially when he was away at night and she was surrounded by the toys and the darkness, she found herself feeling very sad but determined to hold on to what she had. He would always be her wonderful Ernest and nothing would ever change that. The system had taken her mother, her brother and her sisters. No one was ever going to take what was hers again.

The Voice of
Regina Twigg

I was twelve when he pulled me against him in the family music room. I began to struggle. I felt his hands on me and the stubble of his beard. I felt his sweat, and his fast, stale breath. He held me tighter. I struggled. He kept on holding me and pushing himself up against me.

Finally I screamed at the top of my lungs, "Daddy, Daddy, let me go, let me go! Please don't do this, let me go!" There were people in the house and he was afraid I would be heard. So he pushed me away. He had a strange expression on his face and I thought he hated me then.

When school started, I was put in a class with gifted, upper-middle-class children. I had always been deprived. I didn't know how to sit in the living room and socialize, and I didn't know how to study or learn the way other children did. It took me longer to catch on to many subjects, and somehow I developed a math block. I just couldn't do algebra.

When I brought my report card home my adoptive mother was furious. She told my adoptive father to take me down to the basement and give me a beating. So he pulled off all my clothes except for my underpants and bra, and held me down and took a leather belt and beat me.

If he couldn't get me one way, he'd get me another. This time he didn't care how loud I screamed because my adoptive mother already knew what he was doing.

By the time he finished there were bruises from the back of my knees to my waist and from the sides of my thighs to my hips. Every place my skirt covered, he hit me.

After that he beat me all the time. I just assumed parents were allowed to do this. No matter how hard he beat me, I couldn't seem to bring my grades up. No one had ever taught me proper study habits or how to outline.

I had one friend, Janie. Once, after one of the beatings, I was standing next to my locker and crying. "What's the matter?" Janie asked.

I told her. She took me to her house after school and we told her mother. I showed her mother the bruises, and she explained to me that this was against the law and that it was called child abuse. When I went home that night I told my adoptive mother what Janie's mother had said. She got very angry.

"You need a beating, by God," she yelled. She had my adoptive father march me right down to the basement and beat me again, harder than ever. I had big black-and-blue marks with blue welts and deep bruises that lasted for days and days. First they got very, very purple, and then they turned blue.

Finally one day I was doing the dishes. I had cleaned the entire second floor, I had changed all the beds for the boarders my adoptive mother took in and I had washed all the socks by hand. My adopted sister and I were doing the dishes together. We were having a little argument about who was going to dry them.

Out of the blue, my adoptive mother said, "I think they both need a beating."

I was beginning to rebel and this time something inside me just snapped. I looked at my adoptive mother and said, "No, we don't. We haven't done anything wrong, and hitting us is against the law. I'll report you."

My adoptive father tried to grab me, and I began to run. I ran and ran. He chased me all over the house and finally, red-faced and panting, he turned to my adoptive mother and shouted, "Don't you ever tell me to beat her again. I'm not going to have a damn heart attack."

Chapter 7

The Mayses

It was a ready-made family right from the start. The perfect American family that Cindy had always dreamt about. A young mother, a good-looking father, two beautiful children and a nice little house. She had carried that dream around for as long as she could remember. It was always there inside her no matter what role she was in, serving drinks behind the bar, waiting on tables, looking sexy and a little bit hard, greeting cancer patients, talking to their families and taking their histories, or typing up reports on Sundays just like any other secretary. All the while, she carried it with her, the dream of someday being part of a real family. Like the one she'd grown up with. It was the old dream of finding her prince.

The next thing she knew, around the first of March, Bob was looking at all the exposed wires in her old trailer, shaking his head, smiling his beautiful smile and saying, "This place isn't safe. It's a deathtrap, sweetheart. Trailers like this can go up in flames in two minutes. You and Ashlee are moving in with me." Today Bob denies that they lived together before Barbara died.

No one at Tampa General Hospital knew they were seeing each other and neither did either of their families, and of course the Cokers didn't know. Bob and Cindy figured that everyone would take one look at them and think that from the moment they met there was an adulterous affair going on. It was best to keep it a secret until the time was right.

A couple of weeks later the Cokers called, saying that Barbara didn't seem her usual self. She needed a blood transfusion. They were taking her to the emergency room. They thought Bob should be there. He was there when she died later that same night.

Bob had been paying for a burial plot for Barbara in Orlando for quite a few months. While they were all in the hospital in Brandon, the Cokers asked Bob if they could bury Barbara in Wauchula using the Coker family funeral home and cemetery. They offered to pay the difference, so he agreed.

The next morning he was understandably subdued. Cindy found him listening to the Carpenters's song "We've Only Just Begun" and crying. That was Barbara's favorite song.

By afternoon he'd snapped out of it. Not long after Barbara's death Bob called his parents and told them that he was happier than he had ever been in his life. He was in love with a woman and had a wonderful new ready-made family.

A few weeks later Bob and Cindy and the kids took off for Orlando and spent the weekend at Disney World. They stayed in a travel trailer with a cabana at Fort Wilderness and invited his parents, who lived nearby, over for a cookout. While everyone was outside eating, Cindy went inside the trailer to get the salad she had prepared earlier. When she turned around to reach for the oil and vinegar, she saw Bob standing in the doorway with a Jack Daniel's in his hand, staring at her.

"I want to marry you," he said, grinning.

"Oh, yeah," she laughed, putting her hands on her hips. "How about Thursday?"

"Thursday sounds good," he answered. "Can we really?"

She looked at him, surprised and very pleased. "You're serious?"

He nodded and said, "I want to marry you. Are you free on Thursday?"

Her face colored slightly. "I think so," she said, trying to keep her excitement under control. "During lunch hour I am." She wiped her hands on a towel; they were trembling. "How's twelve o'clock?"

He put his drink down on the kitchen counter and grabbed both her arms at the elbows. He threw his head back laughing, then with a wild, joyful yelp, he picked her up, swung her around and carried her outside to tell everyone.

Soon after the wedding there was a knock on the door. Cindy was in the middle of folding laundry, which was spread all over the couch. When she opened the door, Velma and Merle Coker were standing there. Kimberly had already begun calling Cindy Mommy, and it was obvious to the Cokers that she was living there.

Bob came out and explained that they were married. The Cokers were cool but polite. Cindy thought Mrs. Coker had one of those "I knew it all along" looks written on her face. They said they wanted to take Kimberly for a few days to visit Barbara's sister, Kay.

"Not now. We're a new family," Bob said. "And we're trying to get these girls used to each other and give them some kind of a normal home life. For the last year Kimberly has lived out of a suitcase, shuffling between me and Barbara and you and my mom. Ashlee was used to having Cindy all to herself. Both of these kids need the stability of a real family. Kim needs to be potty-trained and learn to feed herself. What we are trying to do here will take some time. We all need to adjust to each other. Not have one kid here and one kid there."

"We're telling everyone the same thing," Cindy added, trying to depersonalize it. "I told my mom and grandparents and brother and sister that we don't want them coming and bringing something for one girl and not for the other. They're both our girls, now. You're free to visit. But just like I told my family, if you bring one something, bring the other one something too. These girls are sisters and that's how we want it to be."

Velma's face got all twisted up as if she were going to cry. Merle put his arm around her, took her aside and spoke very quietly to her. After that they both left.

Velma's worst fears were materializing before her eyes. Since the funeral she had been living with grief beyond words. She had turned her home into a shrine, filling the walls and shelves and mantels with pictures of Barbara in every stage of life. Her beautiful Barbara. Fate had already dealt Velma one cruel blow. Daughters were supposed to bury their mothers, not the other way around.

With her last breath, Barbara had looked at Velma and said, "Take care of this little girl for me, Mother. Raise her for me." And now even this was beyond Velma's control. Her hands were tied.

Sometimes she would see a little girl in the supermarket or out on the street and begin to cry, not knowing whether she was crying for Barbara or for Kimberly. She had lost not just her daughter but her granddaughter too.

Torn by grief and a sense of terrible helplessness, she began sending letters to Kimberly. Cindy was enraged. Kimberly was barely two years old; she obviously did not read or write or even know how to open an envelope with a letter inside. To Cindy, the letters seemed morbid and destructive.

She would open letters that said: "Dear Kimberly, Remember the peach tree [or the apple tree or some kind of tree, she couldn't really remember what] that was in the backyard that you used to look at, sitting on your mother's lap? Well, the blossoms are in bloom now." Or, "We went to the cemetery and visited your momma's grave." Or, "In the church last Sunday, they planted a tree in memory of your mother." Cindy was sorry for Velma, but not that sorry. She'd be damned if she was going to read these gloomy letters to a two-year-old who thought *she* was her mother.

The Cokers called again to say they wanted to take Kimberly to see Barbara's sister. This time they wanted to have her visit with them for a week or two. But they had these pictures of Barbara all around the house and they couldn't seem to understand that Kimberly needed time before learning about her mother. It was their business now, Bob's and Cindy's. When they thought she was old enough, they would tell her.

Another letter arrived. This one was a bill from the Cokers' funeral home for the balance due on Barbara's burial. Bob sat down and wrote the funeral home a very nice letter explaining that this should be sent to the Cokers because that was what they had agreed upon. A few weeks later a letter came back from the funeral home, saying that the Cokers had no such recollection and that Bob owed them the balance. That was the beginning of the war.

The decisive event occurred a couple of weeks later. Bob was in sales and traveled a few nights a week. One of those nights Kay's husband called, asking for Bob.

"I'm his wife," Cindy said. "Can I help you?"

"I'm Barbara Coker's brother-in-law," the man said. "I understand you're not letting Merle and Velma see Kimberly."

Cindy leaned forward and collected herself. She spoke calmly and tried to explain. "This little girl needs a stable home life before she goes packing on another trip."

There was a sudden, impulsive burst of rage on the other end of the wire. "You're not Kimberly's mother!" the man shouted.

At that point Cindy hung up. He called back. She hung up again, but it was too late. He had torn right into her dream.

By the time Bob called later that night she was hysterical. "I could put up with the letters, even the funeral bill. But sweetheart," Bob said soothingly, "these calls upsetting you when I'm away are just too much." The next day they got their phone changed to an unlisted number.

Then Barbara's brother-in-law called Bob's younger brother Reed, trying to get the unlisted number from him and telling him what terrible people Bob and Cindy were for not letting Kimberly visit the Cokers and not letting her know who her real mother was. Reed hung up on him and got his number changed too. For the next three years that was the end of the Cokers. Cindy was relieved. Mrs. Coker had never approved of her and was a thorn in her side, always reminding her that Kimberly was not her baby and that Bob had been married before. Now Cindy could go back to her dream of the perfect ready-made family, at least for a while.

The Voice of
Cindy Mays

Soon after we got married, we went to Daytona Beach for a week with
the girls. Bob's parents and brother and sister-in-law came down for
the weekend. We got there on Saturday, and you know your first day at
the beach you're gung-ho.

Bob wanted to take a ride in an old jeep that did not have an inspection sticker, current tags or insurance. He had towed it behind our car
with a trailer hitch and tow bar.

After he had a few drinks, we left the girls with Ruth and Bob—that's
his daddy's name too. Debbie, Reed and Bob and I went for a ride on
the beach. I was in the front seat next to him, and his brother and
sister-in-law were in the back. The jeep was a four-wheel-drive and
Bob wanted to show Reed how well it drove in the sand. I think Reed
wanted to buy it or was thinking about buying it. Anyhow, Bob drove it
right into the dunes, and when he did, for some reason some people
thought he was trying to run over their dog. They called a police officer
and described the jeep.

We were two or three hundred yards down the beach when this
police officer stopped Bob and said, "Let me see your license. You
don't have a tag, and you don't have an inspection sticker."

Bob said, "Well, yeah, I'm just staying up here and I'm showing my brother how the four-wheel drive works."

"We got a call down at the headquarters. Someone said you tried to run over their dog."

At that point Bob got hostile. I was sitting in the jeep and Bob was standing outside, but I was close enough so that I could see Bob getting mad.

I remember saying to Reed and Debbie, "Oh my God, he's starting to yell, he's getting out of hand." I wanted to get out and go over and see if I could calm him down, but Reed and Debbie told me to stay in the jeep because I was crying. I couldn't stop crying because it was just so upsetting to hear him yelling like that at a police officer the first day of our vacation. I couldn't believe it was happening.

He started to scream, "I didn't try to run over that goddamn dog. You're crazy. They're all crazy." He just became really loud and obnoxious and kept screaming at these cops and they just handcuffed him and took him in and booked him.

I was still crying. I told Reed to drive the jeep back to the motel. The police told us where they were going to take him. When Bob got down to the station they gave him a Breathalyzer test. They dropped the charges of no inspection or sticker and booked him for driving under the influence.

For the first time I thought, "Oh God, what have I gotten myself into this time?" After I bailed him out I just had to get away. I got in the car and left and drove around alone. I left him there at the room with the girls and his mom and dad and brother and sister-in-law. I kept thinking about why this had happened. When I came back, I told him that I didn't want him to sit around and drink like this. He apologized and pretty much curtailed his drinking for the rest of the week. Still, I couldn't get over the fact that he would get so wild and talk to a police officer like that. It was the first I had seen of his temper.

Shortly after that he called me from a Steak & Ale Restaurant, very drunk. He wanted me to pick him up. He had decided to keep drinking with some of his customers.

When I got there he was sitting at a table with a group of people, a couple of women and a couple of men. He was very obnoxious, and I don't remember exactly what he said but he had something very smart to say to me.

There was another woman there who acted like she was interested in Bob, and I tried to just stay calm and say, "Bob, you've had enough. Let's go."

Well, no, he hadn't had enough, so he ordered another drink and he said something else that hurt my feelings. I remember I took the drink and I just threw it all over him underneath the table. With that he jumped up and walked outside. I followed him, but he yelled and cursed at me and wouldn't get in the car. He drove his own car home. I tried to follow him, but I lost him.

I don't know how he ever drove home that night. There was a time lapse of about an hour before he arrived, so I drove the baby-sitter home and waited for him. He eventually pulled up and was stumbling around in the parking lot. Then he stood there and peed right in the tenants' parking area. He was blind drunk that night. He didn't even know I was there, he was so drunk. He might have had more drinks on the way home, I don't know. But when he got inside he just passed out. This was during the first year of our marriage.

[Bob now claims he was not drinking heavily at the time.]

The next time he came home drunk, I wanted to know where he'd been. "Why didn't you pick up the phone and call? Just pick up the phone and tell me that I shouldn't worry that you're dead somewhere," I said.

I should have known not to try to talk to him when he's drunk. It's always better to just let him pass out and sleep it off and feel bad the next day and then discuss it. But I didn't do it that way. I remember that night he was trying to go to sleep and I kept grabbing his arm, saying, "Where were you? Just tell me. Where were you?"

"No, I'm not going to tell you; I'm not going to talk about it," he said. "Shut up, leave me alone. I'm going to sleep."

And I kept insisting, wanting to know where he had been and why he hadn't called.

Bob's usually very scary to be around when he's drinking. But that night at the duplex, he was terrifying. He suddenly pulled a gun on me. A .357 magnum.

"Shut up and get out of here. Get your daughter and get out of here," he yelled, pointing the gun at me and pulling back the trigger.

We had a big four-poster bed and he kept the gun in a holster on his side of the bed, strapped over the headboard post. He was drunk, with a gun ready to fire pointed at me, telling me to take my kid and get out of there. I was shaking. Kimberly was in the bed with Ashlee, but she slept right through it. I picked up Ashlee and ran.

I had come to the marriage with this dream that we were a family, and all of a sudden there he was with a gun pointed at me, saying, "Get your daughter and get out." That sure crushed the dream that my kid was his kid and his kid was mine.

I was still in my nightgown. Ashlee was in her nightgown. I just picked her up and carried her over to the neighbors. This was about one o'clock in the morning. She was six years old.

Bill and Vicky Reynolds, the neighbors, had two children, a girl and a boy. I think her daughter was the same age as Kimberly and the little boy was just a toddler. Vicky was asleep; her husband traveled. He was in sales too. He wasn't home that night.

I started pounding on her door, crying, "Can I come in? I've got to come in. Can I stay here? Please let me in, let me in," I begged. "I need a place right now."

I remember we turned out all the lights because I didn't want him to know where I was. I was afraid he would come looking for me with the gun.

I didn't know until the next day that he had called my dad and said, "Come get your daughter. I kicked her out of here. She's walking down the road somewhere with Ashlee." I didn't even think of calling the police. At that point, I still loved him too much.

The next day I left Vicky's house and went next door, back to our duplex, and got dressed. He was still passed out. I got Kimberly and Ashlee ready, took them to the nursery just like I always did, and then I went on to work. By the end of the day I had roses. You know, he'd send roses, that was his norm.

Those nights weren't frequent, not every week or every month, but I just never knew when it would happen. I still have the little cards that came with the roses, you know; I still have them somewhere in the house. I've got quite a few cards for things like that.

Part II

BEYOND
THE SORROW

> She was in a far
> fiercer mission
> than
> anyone realized.
> With passionate
> single-
> mindedness
> she was
> retrieving
> her own soul.
>
> COLETTE
> DOWLING

Chapter 8

Living Apart

Ernest was restless, even when the children climbed on his lap vying for attention. His eyes were like stones in his head, dull and old.

Regina looked at him from the other side of the kitchen with his face buried in his hands, propped up on his elbows, all closed in on himself. From a distance he looked like the same old Ernest, but she wondered what was happening inside of him and outside in the mysterious life he lived at work, the life apart from her. She felt afraid without knowing why. She sensed that he wanted a change.

Her adoptive mother died unexpectedly of a massive heart attack and left twenty-five thousand dollars. Regina suggested they use the money to buy a new house. She thought maybe that would please Ernest.

They found a three-bedroom, concrete-block house in Orange City, Florida. It had an in-ground swimming pool. The pool had been there for about twenty years. It was twenty-two feet long by twelve feet wide, and it was six feet deep in the middle. Rather than filling it in with dirt they decided to fix it up and enjoy it. Arlena, who had just turned five, loved that swimming pool. She could go into the water with a tube around her waist and she could float all day. For the first time in her life, she could carry her own weight easily.

The whole family loved that pool and the house too, but there were ten of them—Regina, Ernest, and the eight kids. The house had only three bedrooms. Regina tried lining the beds up dormitory style, the way they had been when she was a child in the orphanage. Four boys in one tiny room and four girls in the other just didn't work. There was no room to play or even to walk between the beds.

After a few months, they hired a contractor to add two more rooms. Then Regina had a brainstorm. Ernest had worked hard all his life, she thought. He'd supported his children and done almost nothing for himself. He'd always wanted a garage with a grease pit, a mechanic's pit, so he could do the same kind of work at home that he was already doing in a Sebring garage, mechanic's work, moonlighting for grocery money. Since they were building anyhow, why not add that as well?

She wanted to see the joy in his eyes again. He had been so tired and worn-looking. She tried to reach him with words, but his isolation was more and more difficult to break. So they put in a garage. Now Ernest could work on cars and earn some extra money at the same time.

Most of all, Regina hoped that maybe he'd be happier and stay home more. She knew his hours at Amtrak were irregular and long. She could see he was still preoccupied. Sometimes in her worst moments she wondered if it was that thin, braless woman. She wanted to talk to him about many things, but there was something in his expression and the cast of his face, even in the way he held his shoulders, that always kept her silent.

Because she couldn't approach him she found herself

studying him from a distance, trying to understand his unmet needs and thinking about his life.

Ernest was the sixth of eighteen children. He grew up in a sprawling farmhouse on the outskirts of Indiana, Pennsylvania, which his parents called the ''happy house.'' It had a lot of bedrooms and a big, bright kitchen. His father had wired the house with its first electricity, but it had no indoor plumbing. They had a lovely duck pond and a Great Dane named Fleece. Even for a Great Dane, Fleece was large.

Ernest's father worked as a tire builder at the McCreary Tire and Rubber Company. They struggled financially. They lived high in the hills, grew their own fruit and vegetables, and baked their own bread. Ernest's mother used to bake so much at a time that the whole six-foot table would be filled with pies and cakes and loaves of bread. It was a close family and, from what Regina knew, a happy childhood. The boys hung around together, racing, hunting and swimming. They raised cows, pigs and chickens. All the kids took care of the animals and cleaned the stalls. Only Ernest could milk the cows though, because they were nervous and he had the gentlest touch.

The family was raised on old-fashioned Christian principles. Their father was firm. He'd tell them to do something once. If they didn't do what they were told, they'd get spanked. He wasn't brutal but he was firm. He had to be, to keep control of so many children. Actually, he was a warm, loving person. He was a good father and a very hardworking man.

Ernest's mother was sincere and outspoken. She'd say what she thought and wouldn't care who you were. She was happy and fulfilled with her children. Even many years later, when they were all grown, their baby pictures still brought tears to her eyes. Those were her happiest times, and she always said that she would never trade them for anything. She had her first child at sixteen and her last one at forty-three.

Ernest was a shy child who couldn't stand a lot of noise. He was so high-strung and nervous that when he was in the third grade he developed a condition known as Saint Vitus' dance. His hands shook and he broke out in a rash. It got so bad that they finally had him stay home for half a year. They sent the work home. Sometimes the teacher would even come to the house. She was a very old lady and a lot of the kids didn't like her, but she was good to Ernest. She let him pass that year.

His nervousness made it difficult for him to handle school. He was good at math, but he was a loner who decided early that he wasn't cut out for high school. He left after the tenth grade and joined the air force. At first he loved it. Then everything began to seem repetitious and Ernest got bored.

He serviced power units for military aircraft but never got to fly in them. What he wanted to do most was to go overseas, either to France or Japan. He put in for transfers several times, but he never got them. At reenlistment time they said they wanted him to reapply for foreign service. By that time, he wouldn't have reenlisted even if he could have gone to England, Japan or France. He just wanted to get out and come back to the civilian world.

Ernest met Regina shortly after his discharge. He was in the parking lot of Westside Plymouth in Akron, Ohio. She had come there for her first teaching job, but she was on summer vacation and was working in a plastics plant on the midnight shift. This particular Saturday morning the woman downstairs asked Regina to run across the street and get her little boy an ice cream cone with sprinkles. The ice cream truck was parked in Westside Plymouth's lot.

Ernest's brother Ed worked there, and Ernest was having his new car serviced. When the pretty blonde in the black slacks and powder blue top walked across the street, she caught Ernest's eye. He drew in his breath and whistled. "Hey Regina, come on over here," Ed called. "My brother wants to meet you. He hasn't seen such a pretty girl in a long time." Ernest kept staring at her; he couldn't look away.

"Would you like to go and get something to eat?" he finally asked.

She saw his eyes traveling over her, admiring her. She folded her arms and smiled, feeling like a movie star. "I'm too tired," she answered. "I worked all night and I didn't get any sleep. Call me later in the week if you want. I'll see what my schedule is."

Regina had dated a couple of guys. In fact, she had grown close to one. A handsome boy, six feet tall. After three months of dating, he left her for his old girlfriend. Now she figured all the boys would hurt her.

But when Ernest called, Regina was surprised and happy. She agreed to go out with him on Saturday night. Everyone went out on Saturday night, she reasoned. It would be good to relax.

They went to a little place called the Glens and sat in a booth eating potatoes and shrimp with hot sauce. Afterward, when they walked through the town, she could feel his arm pressing against hers. They went to a lounge on Market Street. A band was playing and they danced. He held her very close. He seemed sure and strong. After that they went out together every night.

Usually they ended up at Regina's quaint first-floor Victorian-style apartment. The bed was built into the closet, which turned around so the bed could fold down. A charcoal sketch of her old boyfriend still hung on the wall. "Are you gonna leave that up there forever?" Ernest asked.

"I haven't decided yet," she answered, laughing. But when he went home that night she took it down.

The next night she cooked dinner for him. The dishes were still in the sink and Ernest was getting ready to wash them. "Regina," he said, "I want to ask you something." He walked toward her and pulled her up from the chair into his arms. "Regina," he repeated. She could hear a breathless catch in his voice. "Will you marry me?"

She told him she wanted to think about it, but her heart was pounding. He loves me, my God, he really loves me. At that moment the realization that a man cared about her and wanted her seemed like the most amazing thing in her life.

Ernest was exactly what she needed. Sometimes he looked at her with the eyes of one dazzled by a beautiful woman, and she could feel him wanting her. When she became a frightened little girl with fear in her eyes, he loved her just as much. He was moved by this, by her sadness and her vulnerability. She felt the unspoken acceptance. Ernest, too, had been made fun of as a child. His family was poor. They suffered hardships together and were very close. Ernest could give her a man's love. He could also give her the large, ready-made family she had longed for all her life and never had.

December 23, 1966, the day of their wedding at the First Christian Church of Youngstown, Ohio, was one of the happiest days of Regina's life. He was twenty-two; she had just turned twenty-three. It didn't matter to her that they didn't have any money to go on a honeymoon. They took a one-night trip to Ripley, New York. There was snow up to their knees but it was beautiful. When they stopped to help a man stranded in the storm, Regina was so excited about being married that she kept telling him her name was Mrs. Ernest Twigg. The man just looked at her like she was crazy. Finally she laughed. "We were just married yesterday," she said.

Regina Twigg was no longer alone in the world. Finally she

had an identity, a connection. There was someone who cared for her and someone for her to care for in return.

They got a loan and bought a used trailer. Turquoise blue with a pink interior, no heat and no storm windows. They survived the winter by running the only electric heater they had, nonstop, in the back bedroom. That was where they stayed. Life in the trailer centered around the heater and the bed. Regina could leave it only long enough to run to the bathroom or to grab something to eat. They bought one storm window at a time out of their paychecks.

She was deliriously happy. If Ernest left the house without kissing her goodbye, she'd run down the driveway after him, barefoot in the snow.

Life with Ernest in Doylestown, Ohio, in that rusty trailer heavy with ice in the dead of winter, was the nearest thing to heaven that Regina had ever known.

Ernest might just as well have ridden up on a white horse and carried her off to his castle. It wasn't just what Ernest actually was, it was what she needed to have him be in order to fill the void in her life. He was *her* man. This tall, gangly, rough-hewn, country boy with eyes like half moons and a smile that started slowly but kept on spreading until it lit Regina's spirit with a love as intense as the deprivation that bred it.

As Regina saw it, he was skilled in the ways that men are supposed to be skilled, the ways that make the world work. When they were first married, Ernest worked for Transformer Service of Ohio. He serviced the high-voltage electrical transformers that produce power for the town. Ernest would be away for two weeks at a time, climbing on those wires. They wouldn't give him life insurance because the risks were too great.

While he was gone she'd miss him terribly. Sometimes she'd almost be overcome with loneliness. When he came home, they'd celebrate for hours. Each parting was a loss, each return a reunion that intensified their passion.

Regina became pregnant in February. She began bleeding during the second month but didn't realize the danger and kept on working. She hemorrhaged and lost the baby in June.

The next winter she became pregnant again. This time when she began to bleed she got into bed and stayed there. Even after the bleeding stopped she was so careful that she barely walked. When the pregnancy was well established, the girls in the trailer park had a baby shower for her. They gave her a set of receiving blankets. She thought they were the loveliest blankets in the world. She treasured them, as she treasured every moment of this pregnancy.

In her eighth month, they sold the trailer and moved into their first home. It was a two-story house in Rittman, Ohio, with big, bright rooms. They painted it green. It had a wooden garage, two big bedrooms upstairs and a small one downstairs. In their dining room was a crystal chandelier that the previous owners had left behind.

Ernest held Regina's hand all the way to the hospital. In those days, they wouldn't let husbands into the delivery room, but he came to see her right after the baby was born. "She's the most beautiful baby I ever saw," he said, "and you're a beautiful mother." For the next three weeks, he carried her up and down the stairs because she still had a tendency to hemorrhage and the doctor told her not to climb stairs.

Ernest switched to Consolidated Freightways Trucking Company, where he was a night-shift dock worker. But Ernest and Regina craved a normal family life with regular daytime work hours, so he began working as an electrician's helper, then went into air conditioning and heating under the GI bill. He finally got a chance to work with Amtrak. Since the hours were better, he switched again.

From that time until now she thought he was happy. He loved their growing family as much as she did. With the birth of each baby he grew a new beard. A symbolic fertility ritual all his own. Even after Arlena's illness they had rejoiced at the birth of two more baby boys, Tommy and Barry. There were struggles, of course, especially financial ones, but except for Vivia's death and Arlena's illness, he had seemed fulfilled. This current crisis was different. He seemed to be withdrawing into himself more and more.

Finally he came to her. His voice sounded strained. "I've got a chance to transfer to the reservation bureau in Fort Washington, Pennsylvania. I think it would be a good experience for me. What do you think? I haven't worked that line yet."

"You've been a commissary clerk and a ticket clerk. You've worked for the AutoTrain," she said, struggling with this new decision, backing up until she hit the wall and felt her panic hard against it.

"But I haven't worked the reservation bureau," he repeated. "I'll be working the computer with earphones. It will be a real challenge. You'll have to stay behind until the house is sold, but after that you and the children can come. The hospital near there in New Jersey is one of the best, if Arlena needs to have surgery."

She looked at him. She saw his expression and knew that he was leaving. Her face became sad and submissive. So this was it—she would remain behind without him. She nodded obediently and watched him walk toward the kitchen for a drink of water. She looked at him as she had so many years earlier when they first met and saw again the broad shoulders that she loved so much, stooping a little now.

The bond of their love was still a mystery to her and yet it was permanent. Their lives and histories were forever entwined. She could not imagine herself apart from this man.

Living alone in Florida with all these children was almost incomprehensible to her.

The old panic rose in her: He's leaving. What if I can't sell the house? Oh my God, he's going away. With effort she calmed herself.

"The Deborah Heart and Lung Institute is a really good hospital. I know they can take wonderful care of Arlena," she said. Then she held out her arms, and he came and sat in front of her on the floor and rested his head on her lap. She put her hand on his hair and stroked it. She bent over and kissed the soft curve of his neck. She had always missed him so terribly when they were apart.

Years earlier, in the trailer, she would sometimes lie alone in the bed and listen to the sound of the icicles dripping in the afternoon sun. Finally, when it grew dark and the icicles froze again, she would get up and make herself dinner. She had no children then, and only a limited number of things to cope with. Sometimes just washing the clothes or singing the songs she loved calmed her. Doing those things made her feel that there was a tiny corner of the world that she belonged in and that she could keep watch over until Ernest returned.

In the early years with Ernest she had moved away from the fears of her childhood, the time when everything was beyond her control, to the realization that she was part of a larger world. She read newspapers. She listened to news reports. She went to college. She taught school. She was a mature adult, but her sense of calm and personal well-being still came from the manageable, ordered little world that this trailer encompassed and that she shared with Ernest.

She was right. Life in Orange City without Ernest was different. The house was huge compared to the tiny trailer, and now there were eight children needing her and counting on her.

Much as she loved these children, much as they were her life, without Ernest asleep in the bedroom the house felt empty. This barren, lonely emptiness clashed violently with the noise and chaos of eight children demanding her attention, needing her, especially when five of them came down with chickenpox at the same time.

She could not even go to the bathroom alone. Yet without Ernest there she felt utterly isolated. Nothing seemed complete. She knew he was working seven days a week, twelve hours a day, trying to meet the expenses of a divided family. Paying rent, buying food and gas in Pennsylvania, while she was trying desperately to pay the utilities and keep from going under in Orange City.

More and more often the blissful tenderness she felt for the children was overshadowed by the emotional and economic responsibilities that weighed her down. Ernest had restored her and kept her balanced. Now she had lost that moment when he would come home from work, open the door and take over with the children—the period, however brief, when she could return at least spiritually from the children to herself because Daddy was in the house again.

The children sensed her weakness and tested her over and over again, pushing against their new boundaries. Even if they were happily playing or watching TV, or eating dinner, as soon as they saw her pick up a newspaper or answer the telephone they came running. As soon as they felt her sliding into a world of her own, a world that did not include them, one of them would interrupt. Sometimes the entire army of eight would pull at the telephone cord, hit the piano keys, ask for help with homework or claim they were hungry, even if they had just finished eating. Then her frustration would surface, only to be followed a minute later by kisses, bitter self-blame and new appreciation of their beauty. "I do love you. I do love you," she would say to each of them. Somehow she had begun to feel that love itself had made her vulnerable and that it was in the enormity of love that suffering lay.

For a while, even without Ernest, Arlena seemed to thrive. Her health was largely unaffected by his absence and Regina's crisis. One day, when she was playing outside with her brothers and sisters in ninety-three-degree heat, Regina began thinking, "I need to get her in here. Arlena can't stay out there. It's too hot out there. Something is going to happen." Somehow she got sidetracked, and Arlena was out for about another hour. When Regina finally got her in, Arlena said she didn't feel well.

They needed food for dinner. Regina started out for the store because she thought that if Arlena would just sit in the stroller and relax she'd be fine. But on the way Arlena suddenly doubled over and screamed in agony from lack of oxygen to the brain. Regina put her hand on Arlena's heart. It was skipping, beating four beats, then skipping the count of two. For a minute it started pumping again, but then it stopped, then started, then stopped.

Wild with fear, Regina rushed home and put Arlena into bed. She was afraid to move Arlena, even to take her to the hospital, afraid she'd die in the car on the way just as Vivia had.

She put Arlena down on the couch and sat at her side and held her hand. "You're going to be okay," she whispered over and over, until it sounded like a prayer. Although Arlena was gasping and weak and very, very blue from lack of oxygen, Regina could tell, as she sat there using a stethoscope the first pediatrician in Sebring had given her, that Arlena's heart was stabilizing. She gave Arlena the digoxin and monitored her heartbeat to see if it was returning to normal. After a while it stopped skipping, and Arlena started to pull out of it.

Arlena closed her eyes and lay there. She looked at her mother once in a while with the tired eyes of a child who had come to expect suffering and weakness. For a long time she didn't have the strength to say anything. Finally she squeezed Regina's hand very gently and whispered, "Thank you, Mommy."

The Voice of
Regina Twigg

Once when I was very young, my adoptive mother bought me a beautiful dress, and I thought she loved me. It was the kind everybody else
wore, a pinafore. I put it on so she could pin it and hem it. I was so
delighted that I began jumping around with joy. All of a sudden she
shouted, "Take it off. I'm taking it back because you can't stand still."

I cried and cried and begged and apologized, but she wouldn't
give me another chance. She just took out all of the pins and took it
back.

Sometimes she could be good and cheerful and caring and moth-
erly, then suddenly she'd lash out at me. The sad thing was that in
spite of everything I loved her, and the way she treated me always
made me feel there must be something wrong with me.

During those years I was haunted by the memories of my real mother
and my twin sisters as little children dancing and playing on the playground at the orphanage, with their strawberry blond hair shining in the
sunshine.

My adoptive parents resented it if I ever talked about my past. They
wanted me to cut myself off from it and forget it ever existed. When I
was nine years old they changed my name from Mary Lee Madrid to

Regina Iris Burge. They pressured me into agreeing, because I wanted to be loved. I didn't have my sisters or my family anymore, so I went along with whatever they asked, whatever they wanted me to do. I knew that I was really Mary Lee Madrid, and I still am, even today. It didn't go away just because they wanted to wipe it out of my life.

If I ever asked about my mother or my sisters or my brother, they'd say, "That's over with. That's part of the past. If you love us, you aren't going to be talking about those kinds of things. You're not going to be asking questions if you love us."

I was trying to be the good little adoptee who would have kissed the ground they walked on just to get a pat on the head. But no matter how hard I tried, it didn't work.

My adoptive mother continued to be on again, off again. My adoptive father continued to beat me and degrade me. Their emotional ups and downs kept me constantly off balance. I'm not saying that I always did everything right or that I didn't sometimes deserve to be punished, but I never knew when to expect it or how bad it was going to be.

If my adoptive mother was helping me with homework and I didn't understand something, she would suddenly hit me or pull my hair like she was trying to rip it out of my head. Then she'd push my face into the floor the way you push a puppy's face when you're housebreaking it.

Once when I came home from school I had just walked a mile and a half and I was exhausted, so I lay down on the bed thinking I would rest a few minutes before I changed the curtains. When my adoptive mother came in and saw me resting, she picked up the curtain rod and hit me so hard that she bruised my whole upper arm.

That weekend we went to a church retreat. She was standing right next to me. Someone noticed the enormous bruises and asked what happened. I looked at my adoptive mother, then back at the women. "She hit me," I said. That was the last time it ever happened.

To the day she died, all I ever wanted was her love, but I never knew how to get it. I loved her with everything I had and cried and cried when she died. I honestly think a part of her wanted to love me, but there was a part of her that just couldn't do it. I think she was afraid that she'd be hurt.

Luckily my adoptive grandmother lived with us. She was afraid to openly interfere with my adoptive parents, but she helped offset my feelings of inadequacy. She told me I was worth just as much as anybody else and she made me determined to prove it. She used to talk to me about being proud of who I was.

"You don't have to take second place," she'd always say. "You're worth just as much as anybody else. Hold your head up high and be proud of who you are."

I decided to try. We lived right across the street from a university. My grandmother offered to help with the tuition and I decided, "Well okay, I'm going to go."

Actually, I paid for all of my college myself, except for one semester. I was determined to do it. I thought if I succeeded I'd have some kind of basic way to support myself. I'd always be able to stand on my own two feet. Being independent was extremely important to me. It was my biggest motivation. It was my way of coping with the insecurity of my early background.

For four years, I almost never went out. It was full-time study, study and work. I wasn't very good at science and math, but I was determined.

My adoptive grandmother gave me the courage to do it. She wouldn't show me a kindness one minute and turn around and shut the door in my face the next. She was always there. She believed in me and helped me to believe in myself.

As a young girl, when I would go to bed at night she'd tell me stories about when she was young. She would talk to me about right and wrong and the experiences of her life. She'd talk to me about things that she went through that would help me grow to be a better person.

By the time my baby Vivia died, my adoptive grandmother had lost most of her memory. I came to the nursing home to tell her what had happened, and I was crying. I said "Grandma, Vivia died. My baby died." She just looked at me. Her eyes were blank and unresponsive.

She couldn't understand what I was saying. It was so hard, because she was my only friend. All those years that I was growing up, my only real friend. Yet, strange as this sounds, I grieved more for my adoptive mother when she died than I did for my grandmother. Maybe it was because I was still waiting to hear her say, "I love you." And she never did.

Chapter 9

A Ready-Made Family

In between fights, Bob was a real performer. He worked very hard to please Cindy, not just in bed but in the everyday things. For a few months, near the beginning of their marriage, he was out of work because his sales had dropped. That meant he could come around to the hospital two or three times a week just to take Cindy out to lunch.

They'd be driving along and all of a sudden he'd say something like, "Hey, babe, is my wallet down there?" Or, "Damn, I lost my spare keys." And when she'd put her hand under the front seat, she'd find a bottle of perfume or a sexy little nightie. After a while, even before he said anything, she could just look over at him driving, his eyes all shiny and his head bobbing back and forth with excitement, and tell that a surprise was coming.

Bob loved surprises. Sometimes a new idea would hit him so fast he even seemed to surprise himself, like the trip they took to Vail.

One Monday morning he called Cindy at the hospital.

"You need to get off work Thursday," he said. "We're flying to Vail, Colorado."

Cindy figured that they spent fifteen hundred dollars more than they would have for the same vacation if they had planned it out in advance. She had always been taught to save, but that was Bob; whatever the issue it always came so fast it made her head spin. Cindy wasn't complaining; she loved that trip to Vail. It was one of her best memories, definitely one of the good times. They were there for four days. The kids were about five and seven. She still remembers how good it felt when she and Bob were going up the lift arm in arm.

"You sure are a handsome man," she'd say, tickling him through his ski jacket. "You really look great with sunglasses and a windbreaker and all."

Bob had learned how to ski in the service. He'd done it in Europe, but Cindy had never skied a day in her life. In Vail, the kids were in ski school every day, and Cindy thought they looked just adorable coming down the slopes with all the other kids in their little group. At night they slept like angels, they were so tired from skiing all day.

Kimberly was especially good at it. She was so lean and athletic. It was the same way with swimming; she loved the water and had no fear of it. She caught on right away. Cartwheels, too. Sometimes Cindy thought she'd be great in gymnastics.

One day, Cindy asked her what she wanted to be when she grew up, and Kimberly surprised her by saying, "A maid, just like you."

"Well, okay, a maid," Cindy said. "But I'm not a maid." She figured Kimberly got this idea because all Kimberly ever saw her doing at home was cleaning and cooking and picking up things.

Just the same, whenever Cindy daydreamed, she always

seemed to remember the vacations, the little gifts, the good times that they'd had with the kids. And the romantic times she had with Bob when they were alone. Everything was great when they were not at home. She still thought about the candlelight dinners they had on that trip to Vail, about the shopping they did and the bottle of special cologne he bought her.

Whenever Bob went on the road or to a meeting, he always brought her something. When he was gone, he would always call and tell her how much he loved her and missed her.

Then there were the silly, wonderful things they had between them. Sometimes he would get into bed at night, pull her up against him and stroke her hair and whisper, "I love you more than all the oxygen in the world," or, "I love you more than all the water in the world," or, "I love you more than every blade of grass in the world."

Whenever she thought about those things, she'd realize all over again that there was a part of her heart that probably still loved him, even now.

Her birthday was December 24, and he always sent a Christmas arrangement to the office for it. She felt proud when it came and all the girls in the office gathered around to admire it. The next day, she'd use it for a centerpiece for the Christmas dinner. It always had holly and Christmas ornaments on it and it always smelled so good. Even though she expected it after a while, she was still delighted and still felt surprised every December 24 when it arrived.

Bob also surprised her when it came to buying a car. One day he decided he wanted a Camaro Z28 T-top, a car with a really big engine. He picked it out at the car lot and made a deal with the salesman to buy the car. After that he called Cindy up. "Hey, honey, let's go out and look at cars today," he said. "Go over to the bank first and make sure that we qualify just in case we find one we like. If we do that," he told her, "we'll have the cash and be able to say, 'Here's the deal we're going to present you with. Take it or leave it.' "

Cindy went to the bank, then down to the car lot. They were looking at all these cars and suddenly Bob said to the salesman, "I like that one. I want to make you an offer. I'll give you a check right now for $12,000 for that car there."

The dealer smiled and winked and said, "I'll take it." Cindy just stood there, dumfounded. It turned out that everyone in the dealership was in on it. He told them it was a surprise for her.

It was a fast car and it was pretty to look at, but it wasn't her idea of a family car. That was typical for him; that's how he was. He found the car he wanted then turned the whole thing around, saying, "Look what I'm giving you."

It was no more than two years later that he did it again, but this time he didn't even bother pretending. He got a boat, but he couldn't pull the boat trailer with the T-top. So he went to a car dealer and picked out a Blazer, then called her up and said, "We're trading in the T-top. I made a deal. Come down to the Chevy place and sign these papers when you get off work because I need something to pull the boat." He already had the deal completed by the time he told her. The payoff balance and everything. They traded the T-top in just so he would have something to pull his boat with. Sometimes she wished he would consult her, but that was what she called his "good behavior," and of course he couldn't be on his "good behavior" all the time.

The Voice of Cindy Mays

I kept telling him that he hit her too hard. There were bruises on Kimberly's rear end from the spankings he gave her. Bob didn't realize his strength when he got angry. Kimberly was very small, and she was frail. She was just a little kid, and he didn't realize his strength when he was sober, let alone when he was drunk.

I tried to stop him, and I know this might sound contradictory because of what I said about how I wanted to be a happy little family. When it came right down to it, Bob would always tell me, "Kimberly's my kid and I'll do whatever I damn please."

Little things used to irritate him. Like when Kimberly and Ashlee would get home from school, they were supposed to hang up their clothes or put them in the hamper. But Kimberly just shoved everything under the bed. I mean she didn't want to hang up anything, she didn't want to fold anything, it just went under the bed. And you know, I bought the girls expensive dresses, and I'd say, "Kimberly, hang your dresses up. How many times do I have to tell you?"

And Bob would hear that and say, "You don't have to tell her more than once." Then he would start whipping her. He thought she was just being lazy and that was a sign of her being lazy.

When Kimberly was around four, before she had her tonsils out, if we'd have steak or chicken or pork or whatever, we'd sit there while Kimberly would chew, chew, chew and chew. I mean it was like this piece of meat was getting bigger and bigger, and he would just go into a rage.

"Kimberly, can't you swallow that goddamn food?" he'd yell. He would just scream at her, right at the table. I mean our meals were just a nightmare because he would scream at her. He made me a nervous wreck.

I can imagine how Kimberly felt if my nerves were on edge as bad as they were. Sometimes he would tell her to leave the table and go to her room, then he'd follow behind her and kick her as she walked, all the way to her room.

Anyway, Kimberly's nose ran all the time, and we used to just sort of joke that she had a terminally runny nose. She would just sit there, and you know, she'd be crying at the table, with her nose running and the dinner in front of her and Bob screaming, and I wouldn't know what to do or what to say to this man.

She ended up with tonsillitis a couple of times, and I wasn't real happy with our pediatrician. Finally, I asked him for a referral to a specialist, and he ended up referring me to an ENT man. I went in to talk to the doctor and said, "Kimberly has had this runny nose as long as I've known her, ever since she was two years old."

He looked in her mouth, moved her head from side to side and said, "Does Kimberly chew a piece of meat for thirty or forty minutes?"

I said, "Yes."

And he said, "Does it seem as if she is never going to finish chewing that one piece of meat?"

And I said, "Yes."

And he said, "That's because this kid desperately needs her tonsils and adenoids out. She has the worst case of tonsillitis I've seen in a long time."

All these years Bob had been screaming at her, when it was a medical problem. I went home and told him but it didn't seem to faze him.

He didn't seem to be sorry that he had punished her over such a long period of time for something that was not under her control. No remorse about whipping her with a book till she was black and blue, or telling her all those years how lazy she was, or kicking her and making fun of her. He just thought all this was being lazy.

[According to Robert Mays, the disciplinary techniques he used for Kimberly ranged "from a pat on the bottom to 'Go sit in your room,' or taking away of TV privileges, or dessert, or something along those lines."]

When she finally had her tonsils out, he wasn't there. I took off from work. I was there in the waiting room all by myself, and I thought that was terrible. He said that he had spent a long time in hospitals with Barbara waiting in those waiting rooms and he didn't want to be there because of that.

Then, when Kimberly was in the first grade, she began to write all her 2's backward. I don't think it's unusual for a child to do that. I think a lot of kids do that, but it drove Bob nuts.

One afternoon he was trying to help her make the 2 right. He was in the living room near the front door and I was in the kitchen making dinner. He was screaming and yelling and calling her names, which didn't surprise me because he always did that. He always talked to me and the children like we were stupid. So he was yelling, "You're not that goddamn stupid, you know. You're just lazy and you don't want to do it right."

Suddenly I heard Ashlee scream. It was a horrible, terrified scream. I ran into the room and found Kimberly lying in a heap on the other side of the room crying, and Ashlee sitting there in shock. Bob had taken Kimberly and picked her up and had just thrown her across the room, yelling, "Get into your bedroom till you make up your mind that you're gonna do it right."

Ashlee was hysterical, and I was just trying to keep Bob away from Kimberly. I said, "Leave her alone; I'll take care of this."

This poor little girl just had a problem writing the number 2, but he couldn't understand it that way. For him it was the end of the world, like she was trying to do it wrong. He just went bonkers over it.

She was crying and screaming, and Ashlee was screaming. You know it was a nightmare that time when he did that. I finally calmed him down.

I said, "I'll take care of this. Just go outside, do something. Take a ride, just do anything."

I don't think he'd been drinking. This was his sober behavior. Then I calmed Kimberly down, you know, I just held her and kissed her and loved her and told her to stay out of Bob's way and just let him cool off. She was shaking so bad, she was just trembling in her bed.

Chapter 10

The Mystery

Regina knew that in case of another emergency, Arlena's blood and medical history should be available. So in 1985, when Arlena was seven, she requested her medical records from Hardee Memorial Hospital. Regina also took Arlena to West Volusia Memorial Hospital for a blood test. The hospital staff told Regina that Arlena's blood was type B. She knew that her own blood was O negative and Ernest's was O positive.

"There must be a mistake. That's impossible. Test her again," Regina said.

The results didn't change, but this time the lab technician explained that maybe the medicine Arlena was taking to keep her heartbeat regulated changed the appearance of her blood type.

Regina rolled her eyes. "What will my husband think?" she said. "I don't know if he'll go for that. He's just a regular guy. One of those old-fashioned people who think black is

black and white is white. And you don't get a B from two
O's."

The technician shrugged. "I can't help you with that," he
said, but there was something in his tone and in his gaze that
made Regina feel that maybe he too was wondering.

Regina didn't tell Ernest. She was afraid of doing so, especially over the phone, because she didn't know what he
would do or think after they hung up. Instead, she began to
ask other people.

First she went to Dr. William Bell, the pediatrician in De
Land, which is right next to Orange City. Then she asked Dr.
Arthur Raptoulas, Arlena's cardiologist in Orlando, Florida.
She also talked with Professor Richard Green at Daytona
Beach Community College, where she was taking a course on
human growth and development for her teacher's recertifica-
tion. The whole class was discussing the embryo, so she
raised her hand and asked how this discrepancy could happen. Dr. Green couldn't give her any answers. Dr. Bell didn't
know. Dr. Raptoulas didn't know. No one ever thought of
suggesting a baby switch. Each time Regina asked, she
thought she saw a look in their eyes, a look that questioned
her integrity. A look that said, "Come on, lady, who else
have you been sleeping with?" It wasn't their fault. They said
they did not know what to tell her. They never suggested
that she was unfaithful, but they never suggested genetic
testing either.

She felt degraded. She believed these people thought she'd
been unfaithful, and that just made her more afraid and more
reluctant to tell Ernest. She knew that he wouldn't be able to
explain it, and she couldn't explain it either. Even the experts
couldn't explain it.

She kept trying to put it out of her mind, thinking, "God,
this is strange. There is no way I can relate to any of this. It
has to be the medicine changing the outcome of the typing. It

must be. There's no other explanation." She had totally forgotten the doubts she had experienced years earlier in the hospital and totally blocked the memories. Her attachment to Arlena was so intense that there was no way that she could even entertain the possibility of a baby switch. At least not consciously—not yet.

I'll tell Ernest when I see him, when we are together again, Regina reasoned, while she was mowing a neighbor's lawn in the ninety-degree heat. She was trying to earn enough money to buy groceries for dinner.

When she finished the lawn, she went home to wash the clothes and hang them out to dry while the sun was still high. For a solid year, she had had no money to repair her dryer. For a solid, endless, interminable year, she had been without Ernest.

Now, as she hung the children's wash on the chain-link fence, just the way that she had every day for more than the last three hundred, she made a decision. "No one has bought this house. It's a white elephant, separating us and making us all unhappy. I'd rather rent it," she thought. "I'd rather give it away, I'd rather abandon it, than go on like this." It was Thursday. She carefully hung the last pair of shorts on the fence then walked into the house and picked up the phone.

She wiped the sweat from her forehead and dialed. "Hello, Ernest? I've made a decision," she practiced while the phone rang. Her voice trembled, but it was not with weakness. "Ernest," she said when he answered, "find us a place. We're coming on Monday."

Chapter 11

The Crumbling Dream

Cindy always said that she would not have a child after she was thirty. It was just one of those pacts she'd made with herself. They'd never discussed having any more children, and she was on birth-control pills for the first couple of years they were married.

After a while she found herself thinking about it, wondering at twenty-seven if she were ever going to have another baby. And if not, what else she would do with her life. Sometime in 1986, when they were in bed one night, she pressed her body against Bob's. Things had been calm for a while and she figured it was a good time. He pulled her closer.

"Bob," she said, "I've been thinking about having a baby."

"No," he snapped. Then, as if he thought of something kinder, he looked at her with a friendly, poster-ready smile. "Cindy," he said, "we have two children and that's enough. We already have two girls to put through college. But there is something else we could do." By the end of the discussion, they'd agreed that instead of having another baby she could adopt Kimberly.

When they went to the lawyer to draw up the papers, the lawyer explained that if something ever happened in the way of a divorce, which there was no talk of at that point, Cindy would be Kimberly's legal, natural mother. When Bob found out he might end up paying child support and having visitation every other weekend, he changed his mind.

"You're not adopting Kimberly," he said. "You don't need to. She's your child, and you don't need a piece of paper to prove it."

Cindy was still so much in love, in spite of everything, and so eager not to quarrel that she agreed to it. She even had her tubes tied, just to please him.

Now that she knew there'd be no more babies, she began to look in other directions. She told Bob that she'd like to take a night class at the local junior college. He seemed to be sitting on the edge of his chair as she told him. He looked at her but didn't make a sound, just sat there listening to the silence.

"Only one course," she said, hoping right away not to set him off.

"It's fine if you want to take that course," he finally said. "But you need to understand that I'm not rushing home to pick up the girls, and I want food on the table, a full-course meal. We're not eating out of the microwave or having pizza. So," he said, pausing for emphasis, "if you can pick up the girls, come home, get the girls situated and make sure dinner is ready, then you can take the course."

"Okay," she said. "I'll do it."

"One more thing," he added. "I don't want to see you with your nose in a book all weekend. I want you to be free to go sailing."

Cindy wanted to take a course in abnormal psychology, even though she wasn't sure why. She signed up, determined somehow to get home from work, pick up the kids, make dinner, and get back across town by seven o'clock. After two weeks of the new routine she ended up in the hospital for four days. It started with severe abdominal pain in the middle of the night. Bob had to take her to the emergency room, where they ran some tests, didn't find anything, gave her pills for the pain and sent her home again, saying she'd be fine the next day. But the next night, as soon as she got into bed and tried to go to sleep, it started again. A couple of times she fell asleep but the pain woke her up.

The next day she went back to the doctor, who said, "If it happens one more time, we're going to admit you." Meanwhile, she was racing back and forth across town to get the kids, cooking three-course dinners, and trying to study on weekends, when Bob wasn't looking. She was learning just enough in the psychology class to know she was starting to resent her situation like hell.

The next time the pains came, they admitted her and ran every kind of test imaginable: upper GI, barium enema, colonoscopy. After all of that they ended up telling her it was a spastic bowel, which meant nerves, too much stress. Before they did the colonoscopy, they gave her a heavy sedative to relax her. She was out of it and hardly knew what she was saying. The doctor wanted her to take her wedding band off. He said something about not wearing jewelry during procedures.

She held out her hand, opened her eyes for a minute and said, "You can keep it, along with the son of a bitch who gave it to me."

After that she quit the course. Cindy wasn't the only one having trouble with school; Kimberly almost failed first grade. At first the teacher, Nora Scott Chadwick, said that Kimberly didn't have a very long attention span, then she decided it was more complex. Wherever the teacher moved Kimberly, even next to the quietest child, she soon had children near her talking. Bob and Cindy began to get called to a

91

lot of conferences, both because of Kimberly's grades and because she was being disruptive in class. Ms. Chadwick told them that Kimberly needed a psychological evaluation.

Bob disagreed. He told Cindy he thought Kimberly just needed to have her ass torn off. Just the same, they went to a counselor and had her evaluated for hyperactivity.

After talking to Kimberly and administering hours of formal tests, the psychologist, Dr. Gerald Mussenden, wrote, "The teacher indicates that Kimberly acts in an odd manner on many occasions and on occasion she speaks to the wall and has said many things in a low tone of voice, which may involve cursing or ridiculing. She feels that other children are calling her stupid. In addition, she feels that they generally make fun of her. It appears that there must be some problems that exist in the home for Kimberly to have the types of problems she is having at school. This must be dealt with directly. This can only be done through family counseling."

Bob said, "No way. Definitely no counseling."

The problems didn't stop. Kimberly ended up failing first grade and going to summer school. Cindy finally took her to another counselor. When he also recommended family counseling, she wasn't surprised. She told him she knew from her own experience how hard it was to concentrate in school with Bob screaming and carrying on at home. Bob still refused to cooperate, but Cindy took Kimberly to a number of private sessions.

Sometimes the psychiatrist would bring Cindy in for the last few minutes and talk to her about the things Kimberly and he had discussed or ask her for a little more background information about how things were going at home. That's when the subject of Solo came up.

Solo came into the picture when Kimberly was three years old. He was her imaginary friend; he was there for her when her rear end was black and blue, when her tonsils came out, when Bob threw her across the room, called her names or moved her to Orlando. She would talk to Solo in the bedroom, take a nap with Solo, and then when she woke up they would play together. From what they could tell, Solo was a little boy. When the teacher called Cindy up and said Kimberly was talking to the wall and to herself, at first Cindy figured she had taken Solo to school. But when she talked to the teacher and found out Kimberly was calling herself names like stupid and lazy, she knew that even Kimberly's imaginary friend had failed to protect her self-esteem. Cindy realized right away where Kimberly had gotten those ideas.

The Voice of Cindy Mays

There were a lot of whippings, you know, when Bob was angry about something she'd done. That's why I ended up feeling I needed someone to talk to and going back to the first therapist I'd taken Kimberly to. I didn't know how to deal with this, and you know, there were other things happening between Bob and me.

I went back to see him and finally I even talked Bob into going. I was very concerned about what was happening to Kimberly. After a few sessions, when we were both in the room with the psychiatrist and Bob was calm, I carefully brought up the subject of Bob's physical strength and the fact that he didn't realize his strength toward Kimberly.

There was a small table in the room and the doctor said, "Well, Bob, with your hand show me how hard you slap Kimberly."

The table was in between us. Bob took his hand and hit the table as if it were Kimberly. When he did the psychiatrist just looked at him and said, "Bob, I should pick up the phone and report you for child abuse if that's the strength you use to slap this little girl. You obviously don't realize your physical strength and how fragile her little body is and how fragile she is. Kimberly is very thin anyway, tiny, and petite."

At that point, Bob just shot up out of his chair, looked at me and said, "Go to hell." He looked at the doctor and repeated, "Go to hell." Then he got up and walked out shouting he'd never be back and that he wasn't a child abuser. So with that the session ended.

[Bob denies to this day ever having abused Kimberly.]

Bob went to the school where the kids were enrolled, took Kimberly out, called his mom and dad and brother and proceeded to pack up and move Kimberly to Orlando. He told the school he was transferring her out and moving her to Orlando with his mom and dad. They drove over from Orlando with their car and a pickup truck to help pack and move Kimberly.

This all took place in front of my daughter, Ashlee, while I was at work. I remember calling the house. The kids usually got home from school at around three or three-thirty. This time Bob was home. That was unusual, so I was suspicious right away. I remember saying, "Let me talk to Ashlee for a minute."

And he said, "Oh, no, she's outside playing."

And I said, "Okay. I'll be home at my regular time, around five or five-thirty."

When I got home, Kimberly was gone. On walking into the house I noticed things were missing, and then I saw Ashlee sitting on the couch crying because Bob had moved Kimberly to Orlando and told Ashlee he was going to put Kimberly in school over there.

Well, it ended up that he didn't go to Orlando himself because it was too far to travel to his job, so he just sent Kimberly over there and had his mom put her in school. He got a room somewhere.

Whenever I called, his parents would say Kimberly was asleep. They wouldn't let me talk to her at all. A couple of days went by and Bob began calling and begging to come back. He said he was sorry about the fight and that he'd go to counseling; he'd do anything to make our marriage work.

I took him back primarily because of Kimberly. Not long after that, there was another episode, and I don't even remember what provoked it. He took Kimberly out of school and went to Orlando with her again. It was just for a few days, but he went through the whole thing of taking her out of school and saying he was moving out and enrolling her in a school in Orlando.

[Bob contends that they were never separated, even for a week, prior to his actual departure.]

When I took him back for the second time, I said, "Bob, if you move out one more time and take that child away from her sister and away from me and disrupt her life, it's over. There will never be any more coming back, because I can't take this and you can't just keep doing it to this child and to me."

Chapter 12

The Family Reunion

Ernest was grinning when Regina stepped off the train with Arlena in one arm and Barry, her youngest, in the other. Four more children were behind her, pushing to get out in front and get a glimpse of their daddy. Ernest reached up and grabbed Regina, and lifted all three of them at once from the steps down to the platform.

"Hey sweetheart," he said.

The very sight of him, the very expulsion of his breath, delighted her. "Oh, Ernest, we're so glad to see you," she said, with the gleeful laugh of a girl, a laugh emerging from somewhere deep inside her. His dark almond eyes lingered on her for a minute. Then he took in the children.

He held out his arms and all of them clamored for a spot against him. It was the Ernest she had always loved, and now she loved him for being there at the train station waiting for them and helping them down that final step.

"What are we all standing here for?" he said with a laugh. "Let's go see the new house."

The run-down white frame farmhouse with the blue trim

was close to the traffic of Route 420. "Come on in, everybody," Ernest motioned, smiling. "Now, it's a little rundown, but it's got two big bedrooms upstairs and a big attic on top of that."

First Regina noticed the broken step leading upstairs and the sagging second floor. Then she saw peeling wallpaper and the plaster falling down in little patches.

"A little work will fix it up," Ernest said.

Regina glanced at the long, narrow living room and walked the other way through the dining room. She saw the dirty kitchen with the double spigots and half bathroom behind it. "A bathroom on the first floor, that's great," she said enthusiastically, ignoring the broken tiles above the sink.

"I know it needs work," Ernest answered, seeing them too. "And there's a lot of traffic. But I was lucky to get it for $625 a month. I just signed up for it yesterday. Someone from Amtrak owns it. Rents around here are really high."

She nodded. "I know that, sweetheart," she said. "This is just fine." The truth was he could have taken her to a one-room hut with a dirt floor and a leaking roof. She'd rather have spread pots on the ground and listened to the water dripping all night than ever be separated from him again. Ernest felt a stab of pleasure. He saw Regina's eyes and knew that she was satisfied.

Chapter 13

Home Life

Bob and Cindy read the paper every day. When they saw that a law had been passed in Florida giving grandparents visitation rights, they knew that it was just a matter of time until the Cokers found them and they were served.

The papers arrived a few months later. At first, Bob said they'd fight it. When his lawyer told him he'd lose, he figured it made no sense to waste the money. So Cindy and he took a picture of Barbara, an old eight by ten, out of a box in the shed, and sat Kimberly down on the couch.

Bob gave her a wide smile and a kiss on the cheek. "Does anything about this lady look familiar?" he asked. Of course Kimberly said no. "Well, we have something to tell you about her and your mommy," he went on. "This lady died when you were two years old."

Then Cindy broke in. "I love you very much, Kimberly; nothing will ever change that. But the lady in this picture actually gave birth to you." At six, Kimberly was old enough to understand that when somebody was pregnant, she gave birth to a baby. "When you were still very small," Cindy continued, "this lady, Barbara, got real sick and she died. But she has a mom and a dad that are still living and they want very much to see you."

Kimberly seemed fine with that. She'd been rolling with the punches for a long time and hardly reacted at all. "Do you have any questions?" they asked.

"When am I going to meet these people?" she said.

At the hearing the week before, Cindy and Bob had already told the judge and the Cokers the happy little family story. "Being as young as they were," Bob explained, "Kimberly and Ashlee were raised as sisters." Then they asked the Cokers, right in front of the judge, how they would feel about taking both girls for the visitation. "See," Bob explained when the judge expressed surprise, "we don't want these girls separated."

The Cokers said that was fine with them, but Cindy was still worried that once they were out of sight they might treat the girls differently, that they might leave Ashlee in the corner, while the sun rose and set on Kimberly.

The Cokers never did that though. They always made sure that if they gave one girl a Barbie doll or a pair of socks, the other got one too. Everyone got along fine.

Kimberly and Ashlee met all the Cokers, and they called Merle and Velma Grandpa and Grandma. And when Ashlee's birthday came the Cokers always remembered to send her something. Once Velma even thanked Cindy over the phone, not just for raising Kimberly but for everything she'd done for her. She said that they could take the girls anywhere. They acted like little ladies, not little heathens.

Bob never said anything more about the Cokers' relationship with the girls. He had a lot of other things on his mind—like the twenty-four-foot motorboat he'd recently bought. Bob wanted to take the boat out every weekend. Unfortunately, that was Cindy's time for settling in, getting the laundry done, cooking and taking care of the kids and house. She worked all week, but Bob wouldn't think of leaving her home on weekends and going boating without her.

It wouldn't have been so bad if he'd only been able to keep his temper. Maybe he could have if the dock weren't always so crowded. It seemed that everybody wanted to go fishing or boating or water-skiing at exactly the same time, and Bob would start cursing and screaming, "They need a bigger god-damn ramp," like it was Cindy's fault.

It was so nerve-wracking if the dock was crowded or the boat engine backfired. She knew it would all come down on her head and she just couldn't stand it. She'd be praying all the time that nothing would go wrong so that at least it would be halfway pleasant to be out there with him.

As she saw it, he had reached a point where the common everyday problems drove him wild, where he seemed to think there was a big black cloud hanging over his head and everything happened only to him. It was the little things that set him off, the little things she knew she couldn't control, that really alarmed her.

One weekend they were fishing in Lake Kissimmee with Cindy's cousin and her husband. Bob had a brand-new, very expensive rod and reel that Cindy had bought him for a birthday present. It backlashed a couple of times when he went to cast with it, making Bob so mad that he threw the damned thing overboard.

But there were still some good times. They still planned meals together, shopped together, and on Friday nights cooked outside, then shared a bottle of wine during dinner. Bob still had that wonderful way about him. People meeting him always came away saying he was the greatest guy that ever came down the pike, so outgoing and vibrant, so affectionate toward Cindy and the girls. Always touching them.

Except for the few people who had actually witnessed Bob

when he was angry, no one knew about his temper. Even Ashlee thought he was a wonderful dad except when he got mad. He did things for her like take her shopping or tell her how pretty she looked and that he loved her. But when he got mad, she didn't want to be around.

"He was like a split personality, a psycho. You wouldn't think it was the same person," Ashlee recalled years later after the lawsuit had become public.

At the start of second grade, Ms. Chadwick, who was Kimberly's first- and second-grade teacher at the Harvest Time Christian School, had called Cindy again. This time she said she was concerned because Kimberly seemed to be developing a wild sexual imagination and a preoccupation with sex. A couple of Kimberly's classmates had told Ms. Chadwick that Kimberly had been talking about sex and penises and a sexual act with a dog. Ms. Chadwick didn't have all the details, just enough to worry her. She got together with Cindy and they talked about it. For the life of them they couldn't figure out where those ideas could be coming from.

The Voice of
Cindy Mays

Another thing I brought up with the psychiatrist is that Bob had an attitude that because this was his house, he could do whatever he wanted to in it. During his showers and sometimes when he used the toilet he didn't like to shut the door. It's like the kids were just sort of there. Like it was a privilege for them to be able to live under this roof with him.

We had two bathrooms, but it was an older home and it needed some repairs. The shower in our bathroom didn't work. So Bob had to take a shower in the girls' bathroom.

I still remember how he explained it. "So what if the door is open," he'd say. "If they know that I'm in there, they don't need to be coming in and out." Or, "If you don't like it, you need to keep them out of there." So he would just jump out of the shower and walk from the bathroom to the bedroom with no clothes on, not even a towel, and this bathroom was in between the two girls' rooms.

No matter what I said, he proceeded to get out of the shower with no clothes on and walk from the shower to the bedroom. That always disgusted me. I always had something to say about it and his remark would always be something like, "Your body is not something you need to hide. It's natural, and if you hide it they're going to be suspicious. Let them see what it's all about."

Of course I tried to keep the girls out of the bathroom but it didn't help that much because he would dry himself and then walk out of there naked, right in front of them.

And he would say, "Keep them out of my way if you don't like it."

Naturally, sometimes they would be in the hall or in their rooms and sometimes I wouldn't be home. That went on right up until the time that he moved out, so Kimberly would have been eight and a half or nine and Ashlee would have been ten or eleven.

I had to be careful how I approached him because that was the time when anything could set him off. A regular, normal, good mood could turn into a black rage whenever something set him off. It didn't have to be a major problem.

For example, we had cattle and there was one cow that continuously got out of the pen. One day when the cow got out, I found Bob in the truck, the company truck, chasing this cow, like he's trying to hit it. He would put the truck in reverse, put it in forward, and chase this cow all around the area where the cow was now penned up again, like he was trying to hit it.

I was screaming, "Stop it, stop it!" The girls just couldn't believe it. They were screaming, trying to make him stop. Finally he stopped, but we actually thought he was going to hit the cow. He thought he was going to teach the cow a lesson.

Another time he built a wire pulley that went from one tree to another and got a chain to put the dogs on it. I guess it didn't work and the dogs got loose. He was in a wild rage over that one. He told us to stay where we were and then he went into the bedroom and got his gun.

We were crying, "Don't shoot the dogs, don't shoot the dogs." He checked the bullets in his gun and I was thinking, "Oh my god, this guy is really going to shoot the dogs. I can't believe it." The kids had their ears covered. I guess he finally calmed down, because he didn't actually shoot them, just scared us all half to death.

Then there was the time with Ashlee. Bob had a rule that the children weren't allowed to answer the telephone when we weren't home unless it was him or me calling. He had this secret code and the kids were told never to pick up the telephone unless it was two rings, a hang-up, then another ring, which meant it was one of us.

But this one time the telephone was ringing and ringing and Ashlee picked it up. It was the Cokers, and when Bob came home he asked if the phone had rung. She told him it had and that she had picked it up and that it was the Cokers. As soon as she saw the look on his face she said, "Oh God. I'm in trouble now."

He flipped out totally. He started hitting her and slapping her all over her bedroom. She ended up on her head, screaming and crying. He was yelling, "Why did you do it? Why did you answer the goddamn phone?" He had just gone nuts.

I finally pulled him off of her and shouted, "Don't you ever hit my daughter again!" Then I cried and cried because now even I was drawing a line between his kid and mine. For me the dream had all but died. I couldn't bear it anymore. He just intimidated people all the time. I guess I felt that if I had no power to prevent him from hitting Kimberly at least I could draw the line with Ashlee.

[Bob denies any violent behavior.]

About that time he kept on telling me that the only person who could ever destroy our marriage and make me lose Kimberly was me. The Cokers couldn't, his mother couldn't, Ashlee couldn't; but if I wasn't careful, I would be the person to cause me to lose Kimberly.

In other words, if I didn't behave, if I didn't keep quiet and accept what he did, he would take Kimberly away from me. He used her as a threat to keep me in line because he knew I had a fear of losing her. He'd play on it, over and over again. I really don't know how to explain it except that when he told me that nothing or nobody could take Kimberly away from me except me, he really meant *him*. He meant that if I didn't shut up and accept his behavior, he had the power to pack up, take her and leave. Just how completely I never understood until it actually happened.

[According to Bob, "There wasn't a tremendous amount of fighting, per se . . . yelling and screaming, that sort of stuff. It was we agreed to disagree."]

Chapter 14
The Discovery

Arlena understood that she had a serious illness, and she clung to Regina for her life. She believed that her mother's strength became her own, that as long as she held her mother's hand in hers or stood close to her mother's legs feeling they were the trunks of two giant trees surrounding her, she would be safe. The magic would work. Even God could not take her away if her mother was there.

This belief gave Arlena the strength to wander short distances. It gave her courage and kept her spirits high. Regina, too, clung to the child, the most vulnerable of all her children. Really, they were bound together, struggling together as if the damaged heart itself made it impossible to cut the emotional artery that ran between them.

The bond was so intense that Regina sometimes felt as if her own soul would be lost, drawn out by her love for Arlena. Somehow by sheer will, Regina seemed to infuse her own life force into this child's frail body. Others who observed the little girl, living and breathing, talking and laughing, glowing, with barely half a heart, shook their heads in amazement. She had such vitality, such beauty, such sweetness that it almost seemed unearthly.

For a long time, her heart and her system seemed to tolerate her condition in a most unusual way. A lot of children with similar conditions were wheelchair-bound all their lives. Arlena not only walked, she danced through life. She could skip, she could jump, she could even run a few steps, and she could climb to the top of the jungle gym and play, play, play.

"Look, Mommy. I'm almost in heaven," she would call, laughing, throwing back her head and raising her eyes to the sky, then shielding them from the blinding brightness of the sun.

By the time Arlena was seven or eight, Regina could tell that she had lost a lot of her strength. "Mommy, I don't feel good," she would whisper, dragging her legs as she trudged behind the others. Regina would pick her up then and feel the warm, soft face and little head go limp on her shoulder. She would look down and see the long, lovely shadows that Arlena's eyelashes cast on her cheeks. Regina did not speak; she just stroked the child's hair, agonizing over her decline and the last remaining hope, the choice between a heart transplant or surgery on Arlena's own heart.

When Arlena became too weak to go to school, Regina knew that her love, her will and all the medication there was had taken Arlena as far as they could. The surgery had to be done soon. Once Regina had come to terms with that, they went to the Deborah Heart and Lung Institute for a consultation and decided, at the surgeon's suggestion, to have surgery done on Arlena's heart. Once again blood was drawn for typing. But this time the information was mailed to them.

Ernest read the letter over and over again. He was baffled and frightened just thinking of it. "How could it be possible?" A nerve twitched in his eye. There was a strange, uncomfortable tightening in his chest. He handed the letter to

Regina. She looked at it; he could see her face flushing. "I should have told him," she thought. In all this time she had never mentioned a word about the blood test to him. But it never occurred to him to ask her if she had known before, to accuse her, or even silently to wonder if she had been unfaithful. The thought itself was inconceivable, the idea incomprehensible. He was too confused and too concerned about Arlena even to entertain it.

Ernest's reaction reassured Regina; at least she knew now that he would not walk out. But at the same time it frightened her because she also knew they would finally have to deal with it.

Regina called a friend who was a nurse. "Get into your car, go to Johns Hopkins and have genetic testing done," she said. "For God's sake, Regina, you can't just wonder if they should use an O-positive transfusion or a B transfusion, and which one would kill her. You *have* to know."

Regina moved her fingers in nervous little circles, twisting the telephone wires around them. She was breathing quickly as if somehow, somewhere deeply buried inside her, she knew that a dark, long-hidden, terrible truth was about to emerge. She sensed it had something to do with Hardee Memorial Hospital, but for the life of her she didn't know what. She still couldn't bring back anything about the first days of Arlena's birth.

"Okay," she said, her voice husky and broken. "You're right, I have to know. I'll take her."

Five weeks later, Wilma Bias, the head geneticist at Johns Hopkins called. "Mrs. Twigg," she said. "We have to talk to you." Regina leaned against the wall. "We can't do it on the phone. You must come to Baltimore, both you and your husband. This is urgent. It's extremely urgent."

They met in the small room upstairs. "There is no easy way to do this," the warm, gray-haired geneticist said gently, turning her sad eyes on them.

She introduced the middle-aged, balding man standing beside her, explaining that he was a psychiatrist. As she spoke, she handed them a written report. "We have proven, beyond any doubt, that Arlena is not genetically linked to either one of you," she said.

Then, moving to the blackboard, the woman picked up a piece of chalk. Her tone was level and matter-of-fact, but the words "not genetically linked" were reverberating violently in Regina's head. She tried to reach Ernest's hand, but there was a seat between them and he was too far away. Ernest's face had turned pale and he was clutching his chest with the hand she needed. Regina gasped, a high, wild, terrified gasp, like a wounded animal who had just been shot, and then she slumped down into the chair, surrendering because there was no escape. For forty-five minutes the geneticist droned on about what the tests had proven and how they had achieved such genetic certainty.

Finally, rousing herself from her stupor, Regina looked up and spoke. "Where is she? Our birth baby? Is she still alive?"

The geneticist was silent; the psychiatrist shifted slightly in his chair. They looked at each other, waiting for the right moment.

"Do you think," the psychiatrist began tentatively, and then he paused to clear his throat. "Mr. and Mrs. Twigg, do you think that maybe if you find out that if she is in a happy home, you might just stay out of the picture and leave her entirely alone?" There was no malice in his voice, just a vague, passionless, dull, droning quality.

Regina felt a little dizzy. Had she heard this man correctly? Was he saying that they alone would learn the truth and live with it? She spoke quickly, holding nothing back. "Are you suggesting that we are not even supposed to let this child know that we are her parents, that we exist?" The muscles between her shoulders ached. "How can we know if she is happy or abused? How can we find out what's happened to her unless we identify her, unless she also has the genetic testing done? Maybe the girls could be like sisters," she added, her voice softening for a moment. "Maybe they could share in each other's lives and visit back and forth. Maybe I could become friends with the other mother." And as she spoke, a long-forgotten image slowly returned and then took hold. An image of a tall, young woman crying in a hospital room, holding a tiny baby wearing only a diaper and an undershirt.

"Oh dear God," she moaned. "She was holding Arlena. That was Arlena before the switch. Arlena was *her* baby."

Part III

SACRED CONNECTIONS

The mother too is discovering her own existence newly. She is connected with this other being, by the most mundane and the most invisible strand, in a way she can be connected with no one else except in the deep past of her infant connection with her own mother.

ADRIENNE RICH

Chapter 15

Arlena

On the way back from Baltimore the old, worn-out 1977 Comet sprung a leak in the radiator, and Ernest had to walk a mile down the road, back the other way, just to get a gallon of water from a convenience store. After that they had to keep stopping every five miles to refill the radiator.

"Damn," Ernest said, pounding the steering wheel once or twice, then accepting it.

She couldn't be like him, always calm, always ready for the next crisis. She wanted to give up like this rickety car. Functioning seemed too difficult, the road back impossible, the road ahead too uncertain. The fear ate away at her, churning in her gut.

"Are you okay, Regina?" Ernest asked in that quiet, steady way of his.

"Yes," she lied. "Only one thing, Ernest. Promise me, whatever happens, nothing can ever change your love for Arlena."

"No way," he answered. "She's our baby."

"No matter what?" Regina pressed.

"Of course not," he said. "No matter what."

Regina closed her eyes and drifted into a troubled sleep. In her dream she was leaving the hospital carrying the baby. She could hear the baby's cry. Something reminded her that she had forgotten to schedule the heel-prick test for the baby. She walked back into the maternity ward through the double doors. The sounds of the baby crying had died away and now she could hear voices and the sounds of celebration. As she approached the nursery window she saw a man standing next to a nurse. The nurse was holding a baby up in the air, and the man and the nurse were both laughing. Regina opened her eyes and wiped away the hot tears. For a minute she stared over at Ernest's strong, dark face still fixed on the road, then her eyes closed again, and again the dream came floating back.

When they finally got home, Regina swept Arlena up into her arms and kissed her over and over again. Beyond everything was their bond. Regina loved Arlena and loved herself as Arlena's mother.

For all the hardships, Regina loved taking care of that angel of a child, and nothing could ever change that. She studied her now, wondering if the sick baby had been given to her intentionally. After all, Arlena was not expected to survive the week. She kept reliving the news. She's not biologically mine, but she's my baby. She's my baby, she's my baby.

Regina had married Ernest and had her babies to end the uncertainty of her life, the confusion, the loss and the long painful search that had made her own childhood so desperately lonely. It frightened her now to think that nothing had really changed. Here she was, after all these years, starting the search for her own blood, living it all over again.

She wanted to slam her fists into the wall and scream with rage at the darkness. Then suddenly she was crying and kissing the child with anguished, wet kisses.

"Mommy," Arlena said, holding her mother's head against her own tiny shoulder. "Mommy, what's wrong?"

"It's just that I want you to feel well again," Regina managed.

"Mommy," Arlena said, as if the closeness of their love, their fusion, had bestowed some strange intuitive sense on her. "Mommy," Arlena repeated, without ever being told anything except that there was some confusion about her blood type and that she would have to be tested again before the surgery, "I don't care if I'm adopted." She repeated the words. "I mean it. I *really* don't care if I'm adopted, because I know my mommy loves me."

Then Arlena followed Regina into the bathroom and stood beside her holding her hand as the water rushed violently out of the faucets and into the tub, filling the room with hot, dense, steamy air that came down upon them like a soft blanket enveloping and sheltering them.

Regina helped Arlena undress and lifted her slender little body into the water. The shock had to sink in. She needed time to process it. It had to become an integral, functioning part of her. Regina looked down at Arlena. Her skin had grown pink from the heat of the water.

No one could be more beautiful than this saint of a child. She valued this child more than her own life. But still, she found herself wondering again about the other child.

"Is she still alive? What does she look like? Where is she?" Regina began trying to imagine the little girl, first as an infant, then as a little one toddling along. Then as a young girl in school. Her mind jumped back to the image of a baby in a frilly dress having a birthday party. "My God," she thought. "She'd be nine and a half years old, not a first or second grader, and I'm still wondering what she looked like in those tiny little dresses that infants wear. Nine and a half. Good God, nine and a half, exactly the age I was when I was adopted."

She closed her eyes and leaned forward, letting her elbows rest along the rim of the bathtub for support. With her fingers spread across her eyes, she felt her mind taking her back to another little girl, one of her twin sisters dancing before her on the playground at the orphanage. "Rosemary," she actually said out loud. "Oh, my baby sister, I lost you too. Where are you?" There was longing and reverence in her voice. "Rosemary," she repeated plaintively. "Where is my baby now?"

The Voice of
Regina Twigg

For thirteen years, I thought my sister's name was Rosemary. After we found each other I learned that her name was Rosemarie. One day the phone rang. I was standing when I answered it, and someone said, "Mary Lee, this is Rosemarie." And my knees, my knees gave way. I couldn't believe that it was my sister.

"Oh my God," I said. "Oh my God." She started explaining to me about who she was and asked me if I remembered her. "Do I remember you?" I cried. "Do I remember you? Oh my God, oh my God, oh my God. Yes, oh yes I remember you." She told me that she and her twin sister were living together and had searched for me; they wanted to see me.

I was going to college at the time and I ran up to my professor that day and shouted, "My sisters are coming. My sisters are coming." They probably couldn't imagine why I was so excited. It was like the sun was shining ten million times brighter. I still had her name mixed up. And this crazy song, "Rose Marie, I Love You," kept going through my head. It just kept coming back to me. I sang it for days. I was absolutely ecstatic. I told everyone in sight, "Oh, my sisters found me. My sisters found me. They did, they really did."

Later I learned that right after high school both of my sisters had conducted a very long and difficult search for me. They had checked out many different records and finally figured out who had adopted me. The state of Ohio had a system that would give you some information, but they would make you sign a form in exchange for it. If you weren't aware of what you were signing and you didn't read the small print on the back of the yellow sheet carefully, you sealed the rest of your family records forever. Unfortunately, in searching for me my sisters signed the statement that sealed the records of our baby sister, Sophie, forever.

I didn't know it yet, but my mother was still alive, and before beginning their search for me my sisters had found her.

While searching through their own adoptive parents' drawers they had come across a Christmas card signed by my mother and sent from a mental institution in Pittsburgh. It was an old card but now they knew that she might still be alive. They were determined to pursue it.

They left their home in Steubenville, Ohio, went to Pittsburgh and tracked her down. Finally they found her still living in the mental institution. Since they were over eighteen they were allowed to sign for her and take her home and become her custodial guardians. They rented an apartment and brought her home to live with them.

When I arrived at my sisters' apartment in Steubenville, Ohio, my mother, my long lost mother, was there, standing in the doorway waiting for me.

She held her arms out and welcomed me. She hugged me and kissed me. We were both crying. And for a moment time went backward and I was three years old again. It didn't matter that I was a good head taller than she. I was still her baby.

"Mary Lee, my little one," she said. "It's so good to see you and to know you again." I just kind of looked at her in total disbelief and studied her and studied her and studied her. I thought, "This is my mother, this is my mother." This is the lady that had me in the hospital, the lady who gave birth to me. This is my *real* mother. This is the mother I longed for and cried for over so many years and thought was dead.

I remembered the love she had for us and I thought about how very much time had changed her. She seemed very, very quiet and very backward, after all the years in a mental institution. There was so much to catch up on. Talking together about our feelings and our losses, and learning about her life, came over a period of time.

In the weeks that followed I learned that my mother was born on a big farm along the Ohio River, just across the river from Wheeling, West Virginia. Her name was Mary Agnes Gura. She had lived a very, very isolated life, the workhorse on her parents' farm. One day as she stood waiting for a bus, Leo Almon Madrid came along and offered her a ride. He was tall and handsome. She climbed into his car. She fell in love with him and eventually married him.

He was the only man that she had ever known sexually. She had always been the perfect little girl on the farm. He dominated her and had tremendous sexual power over her.

First they had twins. Soon afterward they had another little girl named Anna Marie. Anna Marie died at eighteen months of pneumonia. Then I was born.

My father never told anyone in his family, except for his twin sister, that we had been born. They found out about Anna Marie when her obituary appeared in the newspaper with his name listed as father. He had been married before. His first wife had a little girl named Elizabeth, whom they called "Dootie Bug." I've never known what happened to her.

When my father abandoned the family and left for New Orleans, he warned his twin sister, Leona, not to tell any of their other brothers or sisters that we had been born. She never, ever told anybody, and we never saw him again.

Through my mother I discovered that I had family in Wheeling, West Virginia, the place my father had come from. I looked up everyone named Madrid in the Wheeling area phone book and wrote to them. Three of them were my cousins, Gary, Jan and Carolyn Madrid. My father never did try to find out what happened to us. He just vanished. His sister Leona said that he flew to New Orleans and married a woman named Vivian.

When I was tiny we lived in a house along the Ohio River, in Yorkville, Ohio. By this time my mother had married my stepfather, and I can remember her sitting in a rocking chair rocking my baby sister and singing. The baby was spitting up milk, and I couldn't imagine where that milk was coming from. My mother was nursing her, but I thought the milk was coming from under the baby's tongue or somewhere in her mouth.

That house in Yorkville is my earliest memory of my mother and our home. It's ingrained in my memory, etched forever into the shadowy scenes of my childhood. I know now that Yorkville was considered one of the river-rat towns, but what I remember is how wonderful it was.

I also remember my mother talking to a friend once. She was worried about where she would get the money to get groceries to feed us because my stepfather, whose name was Homer Joseph Gibbons, was a chronic alcoholic and an epileptic. He worked in a steel mill in Wheeling, West Virginia. During all the years she was married to him he worked for that mill, but we didn't have enough money to buy food because he spent it on alcohol. He had the money. He just didn't give it to her. I always thought my name was Gibbons until I saw my adoption papers at eighteen and found out that it was Madrid.

My stepfather was very violent. I recall us running out to my grandparents' farm to hide from him because he would beat the living tar out of my mother. He would just beat her up. I remember some of his violent tirades to this day. I remember how frightened she was when she ran to the farm to escape my stepfather's rage.

But more than anything, I remember a sense of love from my mother. My mother loved me; my mother loved my sisters. That bond was there. That's why I know she'd never have given us up if she was not forced to.

Back in those days anyone could sign somebody else into a mental institution, and even get paid for doing it. My stepfather accused her of trying to hurt her children. A preacher whom I met years later when I was already grown and married told me that my mother was a very gentle, beautiful woman who was never mentally ill.

I met this preacher at a church retreat when my oldest daughter, Irisa, was just a baby. He said he was from Steubenville and that he had been the pastor of the church there for a long time. I got the notion in my head to ask him if he knew of anyone named Gibbons. It turned out he knew my mother very well. He had known her for years. He said she should never have been in a mental institution. "Your stepfather was jealous of your mother. He was afraid that someone else would fall in love with her and take her away." She spent fifteen years in that institution because of his jealousy and rage.

As soon as my mother got used to the outside world, we sisters helped her get her own apartment in Morgantown, West Virginia, and readjust to life. She did very well. I have been told that if you weren't mentally ill when you went into one of those places, you were when you got out. But my mother was still functioning.

The beautiful, young, strawberry blond woman with the voice of an angel was now a gray-haired lady, small and a little bit overweight. Her hands shook and she could not stand still. Sometimes she would rock back and forth on both feet. Still, she was rational and she loved to help with the grandchildren. At least she was given the chance to be with her family again before she died.

Just before her death from pneumonia at seventy-two, my mother told me that she had always loved my father. She also said that she had attended a family funeral shortly after she had gotten out of the institution. While she was there, my stepfather tapped her on the shoulder. She turned around and saw him, the one who had put her in the institution. His eyes were dark and melancholy, he had developed cancer of the face, his chin and half his cheek were gone. His face was grotesque.

"It was like a nightmare," she said. "As if the evil part of him had come from the inside out, but it was real." He had actually taken on the appearance of the monster that he had been to her.

Chapter 16

Breakup

Bob and Cindy's last week together was one of the best ever. That was the strangest part about their marriage: It could be pure hell, with constant fighting, and then if they went away together to Jamaica or the Bahamas or on a cruise or whatever, Bob was like a different man. A brand-new lover, passionately courting her all over again.

That's how it was in July just before they separated. The children were in Phoenix visiting Cindy's mother. Bob and Cindy were at the beach. Bob had promised that they wouldn't have to be out on the boat every day, and he kept that promise.

Sometimes they'd go fishing or cruising, but sometimes they'd just lie on the beach laughing and talking or getting the sun and swimming in the pool at the motel. Then they'd have a romantic dinner or take a walk on the beach or bring food in and just spend the whole night being close or making love.

The minute they got home his personality was transformed. It started all over again. Lightning had hit the air-

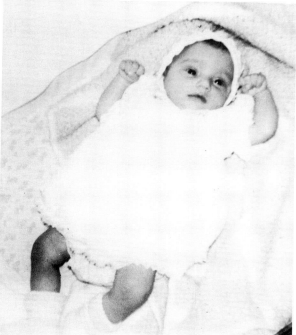

Arlena Beatrice Twigg, about eight weeks old, at home after returning from Miami Cardiac Hospital after her first catheterization.

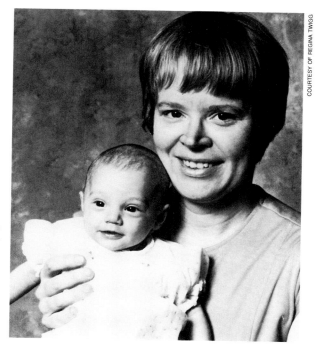

Regina and Arlena, three months old.

Kimberly opening presents on her third birthday.

Kimberly at three and Ashlee at five, sleeping on a ski trip.

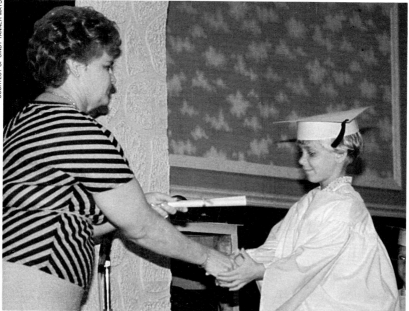

Kimberly's graduation from kindergarten.

The Twiggs in 1984 in their Sebring home. Front, left to right: Ernest with Tommy on his lap, Regina with Barry on her lap, Ernie, Will, Irisa with Arlena on her lap. Back row, left to right: Normia and Gina.

Regina's two sisters Rosalie and Rose Marie and Regina held by her mother before they were put in a children's home. At that time, Regina's name was Mary Lee.

This is the sister for whom Regina is still looking. Sophie, at three, was taken away for adoption in front of Regina on the children's home playground.

Kimberly at two, and Ashlee at four, shortly after Bob and Cindy were married.

Kimberly, age three.

Arlena Beatrice Twigg on her fourth birthday.

Arlena at seven, missing her front teeth.

Bob Mays and Cindy
during happier times,
May 1986.

Bob Mays with Kimberly
and Ashlee at the girls'
last Easter together.

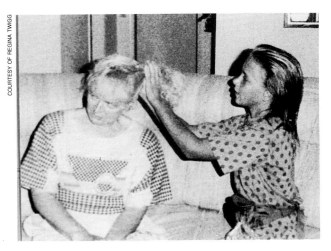

Kimberly fixing Regina's hair, July 1990.

The first visit between Kimberly and her Twigg siblings at the White House Putt Golf Course in Sarasota, Florida, in June 1990. Very front: Barry—Tommy has his arm around him. Left to right in the main row: Normia, Kim, Irisa, Gina, Will, Ernie.

conditioning unit while they were away. When Bob came home and saw the air conditioner he went wild. At some level she felt he blamed her.

"That's it, I'm moving," he screamed. "I can't stand this goddamn house. You can stay here or you can come. I don't give a damn; I'm moving." A minute later he said, "We're selling this house, I hate it. I hate Hillsborough County. I'm moving to Sarasota. I'm buying a place. I'm outta here."

By the time the girls got back a few days later, Bob had already bought an apartment in Sarasota. He told Cindy she could take the marriage or leave it. It was all in her hands. When she reminded him that she would have to travel an hour each way to get to work, he just shrugged.

At that point, Cindy was so sick of living this kind of life with Bob that remembering the romantic week at the beach only made it worse. She felt like she was living with a Jekyll and Hyde personality. No amount of connection, lovemaking or sweet talk ever changed anything. Even the feeling she sometimes had that they were so close, almost one person, didn't really mean anything because it always came back to this.

"Bob," she said angrily. "Three strikes and you're out. If you leave me again, there'll be no coming back. Listen sweetheart," she said, instantly sorry. "People's air conditioners break all the time, pumps spring leaks, roofs need to be replaced. The things that have happened to us with this house happen to people all the time. These are not things you can control; these things happen to everybody in every walk of life."

"Not me," he yelled. "Not me."

She knew more clearly now than she had ever known before that the rest of her life with this man would always be this way.

He still refused to get therapy, he still said she was the one with the problem, and at every turn he still threatened to take Kimberly. She got on his nerves, the kids got on his nerves, the sky itself got on his nerves. In a dazed kind of way, she was glad he was finally leaving. She even helped him pack. The torment would finally be over.

When the girls came home Bob and Cindy sat them down on the couch. It was the saddest day of Cindy's entire life, even though she thought she was ready for it. For seven years their lives had been bound together. She could hardly remember life before Bob. That time belonged to another world. She was thirty-two years old now, and her tubes were tied. But it was not just the man and the marriage and the dream. She loved Kimberly as much as she loved her own daughter, even more, if that was possible, because of all she knew Kimberly had been through.

Bob was talking to the children. His face had taken on that cardboard smile, the salesman smile she had seen so many times before. "I'm moving to Sarasota, sweetheart," he said to Ashlee. "And I'm taking Kimberly. Mom and I just can't live together anymore."

Both the girls began crying and holding each other's hands. Then Cindy started crying. All the arguments that she had with herself about why this was best, all the resolve that had made her glad suddenly vanished.

She promised Kimberly through her tears that no matter what happened they would still see each other and that she would always be her mommy.

Bob agreed and said he would still be Ashlee's daddy. All of them were crying then, hugging and kissing each other, vowing over and over that those things were sacred and would never change.

Cindy can still remember that when he took Kimberly that day she was crying and calling, "Mommy, Mommy, Mommy." She wanted to stay with her mommy. The dream of Cindy's entire life seemed to pass before her. With a touch of doom he led her out of the house, the lovely, motherless baby she had rescued and raised. He put her in the car. She wanted her mommy and he put her in the car.

By evening, Cindy had argued herself through it. She cried and spoke to herself in the second person. "You cannot do this to those girls or to yourself another time," she said. "This is not good for anyone. It's no way to live." The next morning she picked up the phone, called a lawyer and filed for divorce.

Chapter 17

Unacceptable Losses

Bob showed up with a helper and a truck. They began carrying furniture out to the truck. Cindy watched numbly as he took all of Kimberly's furniture, her toys, her toy boxes, her clothes, the gas grill Cindy gave him for Father's Day and some of the dishes and kitchen things.

When he announced that he wanted the big four-poster bed to hang his gun on, Cindy drew the line. She said no and she meant it. After weeks of arguing she said, "If you want the bed so badly come and get it. But by the time you get here my name will be carved across the headboard and every girl you take to it will know who that bed belongs to." After that she never heard another word about the bed.

In the beginning Bob seemed to think it was the same old routine. "Hey sweetheart," he said cheerfully when he called a couple of days later. "I've got a great idea. Let's stay separated for six months and date each other. Maybe that way we won't fight."

Cindy missed Kimberly terribly, and Bob too, but she had made up her mind. "Bob," she said, "do you remember when I told you that if you took that baby and moved out of here one more time, it was over? Well I meant it. There's no dating and there's no coming back."

He called again the next day. "I bought a new sofa, babe, and a love seat, your favorite colors. You're really gonna love them. Come on down and see them."

When Cindy didn't go for that, he brought Kimberly over and allowed her to stay for one night. Kimberly kept saying, "Are you and Daddy going to get back together? Don't you love him anymore? He still loves you."

Then the tears came to Cindy's eyes all over again. Kimberly hated to see her that way; it made her feel so helpless.

"Why don't you just come down to our apartment and spend the weekend with us, Mommy?" she said gently.

Cindy cried and held her. "Honey, I can't," she said. "Daddy and I just can't work it out." It practically killed her to talk to Kimberly like that and cause her pain. She figured Bob had sent Kimberly to talk to her, and now the poor kid was getting caught in the middle.

When he came to pick Kimberly up, Bob backed right into her car without seeing it. After that, he kept crying and saying he couldn't understand why she was so cold. The words stayed with her. She wondered what he'd do if he knew that she had already called a lawyer and filed for the divorce. The thought of hurting him frightened her; she wanted to reach out and touch him. She wanted to comfort him and tell him she loved him, but at the same time she wanted to race away from his rage before it consumed her.

Instead, she just made small talk about getting the car fixed, about getting a couple of estimates to figure out the best price. Then she kissed Kimberly and Bob, polite social kisses that had no feeling, as if they were all characters in a book and the two of them were setting out for a special weekend together.

The day had exhausted her. She fell into a deep sleep filled with tangled dreams, then awakened with a start. The night seemed filled with danger like a big river to be crossed, but she couldn't turn back. She began to shiver and then to sweat.

She wanted him so bad that sometimes it hurt. At the same time she was really scared of what she'd be getting herself into if she backed down this time. She knew how much she loved Kimberly, and in spite of all of her resolve she loved Bob too. She still wanted it to work; she just didn't believe in it anymore. He wrote her a letter saying, "Baby, I think you love me every bit as much as I love you. Please don't give up on us." She resisted.

Finally he offered to go back to the psychiatrist, Dr. Stephen Groff, whom they had seen together after their last separation. He would drive from Sarasota to Tampa just to see him. Cindy started hoping all over again.

"He's not going to continue, Cindy. I know his type. I know what his history is. He'll quit," the therapist told her.

Cindy nodded and made a face that said she understood, but her eyes were pleading with the doctor not to go on. She needed to hope.

Each week, the therapist would say, "Well, he came today. This is good, but don't get your hopes up that he's going to continue."

After a few more sessions it turned out that Dr. Groff was right. Bob got mad about something. "I'm not the one with the problem, you are," Bob stormed.

After that Cindy didn't hear from him for a few days. But then he called again and started telling her he loved her all over again.

"Sweetheart, I still believe we're gonna work this out," he was saying, when someone rang his doorbell and served him with the divorce papers. There was a pause as he rattled through the papers and then an explosion. "You bitch," he yelled. "You little bitch." Then the line went dead.

When her attorney called the next day, he said, "Bob's denying you any contact at all with Kimberly."

"No visitation ever, not ever?" she said, gasping. "He wouldn't do that."

"He's doing it," the lawyer said, not gently, just explaining.

"But I'm her mother, I'm her mother. He can't do that. She needs me." And as she spoke, a cold, slow wave of panic shook her. "He promised when he left. He said he wouldn't do that. He promised I would always be Kimberly's mother and he would always be Ashlee's daddy, no matter what else happened. No matter what else we decided. He swore it the night he left."

"He changed his mind," the lawyer said.

"I'm sorry, Cindy, but you don't have any rights to her. It's entirely up to Bob whether Kimberly sees you or not."

"Bob," she sobbed, calling him at work, crying into the telephone. "Please don't do this." In a daze she kept repeating it, "Please, please, please. Don't do this."

"You're not going to see her again," came his answer, sounding muffled, faraway and full of contempt. "You divorce me, you divorce Kimberly."

"But you promised. I've raised her Bob; I'm the only mom she knows. You're taking her away from her sister and her mother."

"You made the choice, sweetheart," he said in a distant, uninterested voice. "Now live with it." The phone clicked. She beeped him.

"Bob," she said, panicked. "What about Ashlee? You just can't walk out on Ashlee. You've been in Ashlee's life for seven years. You just can't walk away from her."

"It's going to be hard," he said, "but I'll do it." He hung up again.

After that he wouldn't even take her calls. She was out of control now and she knew it, but she couldn't stop herself. She kept on beeping him, one time after another. It was a computerized digital beeper and she had put his number in, so she just beeped him over and over again, while her forehead ran heavy with sweat. He still wouldn't answer. Finally the phone rang.

"I've just had a call from Bob's lawyer," her attorney said, sounding tired. "You're harassing Bob, and if you don't stop he's going to press charges."

Cindy hung up the phone and fell onto the bed in disbelief. She stared blindly at the floorboards and the windows. For what seemed like days, Cindy looked outside through the windows and saw nothing.

The next morning she called in sick and dialed Dr. Groff. She wondered if her body would work long enough to get her out of bed and dressed and into the car so she could talk to him. She needed to explain that this couldn't be allowed to happen, that without Kimberly her life would be meaningless.

"Cindy," he said, looking at her pale face, swollen from crying. "Cindy, your life will not end and it will not be meaningless." He held out his hand to comfort her. "It just feels that way now. You're a strong woman and a survivor. You've got to get past this. You must think about yourself and Ashlee now. You've got to pull yourself together. There is nothing you can do about this. You have no rights to Kimberly; you have no legal standing in the courts. You're powerless. Go home and take down the pictures and the portraits of Kimberly and get on with the rest of your life." She listened quietly, numbly. "You must carry on from here, from this day forward, as if that child never existed."

Her feet ached; her head felt as if it might explode. It was an act that had to be done. The final act, like death, she told herself. An ultimate act that would never be reversed. She circled the house over and over again, staring at the pictures of Kimberly. It seemed like a long walk but she circled around again and paused at each one. She stared at the pictures of Kimberly's third birthday party and her fourth Christmas, and her second-grade class picture.

"This child is my baby, no matter what Bob says, no matter what Dr. Groff says," she said as she removed one picture from the wall, then another.

It was coming to an end but it would never really end. She knew that. "My precious little girl," she said softly as she stumbled toward the shed.

Carefully she placed all the photographs, still in the frames, in a big empty box. Her head ached with an unreal, unclear sense of loss. A husband gone, a baby gone. Was it possible, was this really happening? "I love you, Kimberly," she whispered on her knees, leaning over the box, closing it as though she were closing a coffin.

Then suddenly she was angry and crying. "You son of a bitch," she sobbed as she turned and ran out of the shed, past the bellowing cows into the cold, wet darkness.

Chapter 18

The Fading Heart

Arlena's surgery was scheduled for August 22, 1988, and it was getting close. Regina began to be obsessed with the idea that they would lose Arlena during the five-hour operation. Open-heart surgery to correct the transposition of the artery and the aorta was tricky. The doctors planned to build a shunt, then attach the pulmonary vein directly to the lungs, then insert a shunt to prevent the mixing of life-giving red blood and exhausted blue blood. If they didn't lose her on the operating table, they might wake up one morning and discover that Arlena had died during the night. Maybe she would die right in front of their eyes the way Vivia had exactly thirteen years earlier. The upcoming operation had added urgency to the sense of impending danger. Regina was confronting her worst fears and trying to conquer them.

Regina told herself over and over that they would win this fight. At the same time, just in case, she wanted to grant Arlena's every wish before it was too late. With a grand sweep of her arm, she wanted to make all of the little girl's dreams come true.

Arlena had missed Florida; she missed the swimming pool especially, because she loved to swim. So three weeks before her surgery Regina took her back for a visit, just the two of them. They stayed with friends who had a swimming pool. Arlena had broken her arm in June when she fell across a concrete slab while roller-skating in the park across the street. But even the cast, which had been weighing Arlena down for weeks and putting an extra strain on her heart, didn't matter. Buoyant again, floating in the pool in her little red bathing suit, with her head bent back and legs wrapped around her mother's waist, she laughed with the lighthearted laugh of a child who could carry herself easily again.

"You're beautiful, honey," Regina said, so moved by Arlena that she had to dip her face under the water to hide her tears. Arlena was brave. There was never a braver child than Arlena.

Even the evening before surgery she seemed to feel good and be ready for it. "Daddy," she said in a steady, sweet voice. "I know I'm going to make it. I've got everybody pulling for me and that's how I know." She was holding her sister Vivia's bracelet in her hand. She kept turning the bracelet over and over. Then she said, "This is my baby sister who didn't live. But I'm going to live. She didn't make it, but I'm going to make it."

At bedtime Arlena climbed in beside Irisa. "Sissy, can I sleep with you tonight?" she asked.

"Of course you can," Irisa said. Arlena tossed and kicked and turned over and over again. "Come on, honey," Irisa finally said. "Try to rest. You have to get some sleep."

Then Arlena began to cry. "I'm scared," she said. "I'm scared I'm gonna die."

"You're not going to die," Irisa told her. "You're going to be just fine, I promise." Arlena climbed into Irisa's arms. "You're going to be fine, honey," Irisa said again and again.

"You're going to be just fine." Finally comforted, Arlena fell asleep. She was practically sleeping on top of Irisa, clinging to her as if for life.

The next morning Arlena was scared again. She tried to say something, but she could hardly get the words out. "I want to come home so Gina and I can eat tuna fish sandwiches in the middle of the night and Normia and I can have long talks and Ernie and Will can ride their bikes with me and Tommy and Barry and I can play leapfrog." Then she began to cry. "Mommy," she whispered, "I don't know if I'm going to make it. If I'm a good little girl, do you think God will let me live?"

Regina wanted to say, "Don't be silly. Of course, you're going to make it." But her own fear wouldn't let her. How could she lie to the child? How could anyone really know what the outcome would be? Her head ached with her own sense of helplessness.

"Honey," she said. "You can change your mind. We don't have to do it right now if you don't want to. We'll wait for another time." Arlena held on to her mother's hand and closed her eyes for a minute.

"No, Mommy," she said firmly. "Let's go ahead and get it over with. We've waited long enough."

The song "As Long as I Have You" was playing on the radio. The words floated through the room. Regina bent down, leaned forward and pulled Arlena against her. "I lost one baby," she thought, "and now I know I've lost another who might still be alive. But as long as I have Arlena, as long as Arlena is all right, I can make it." Her large, strong fingers trembled as she buttoned Arlena's coat.

"My precious little girl," she said, amazed all over again by Arlena's bravery and maturity.

Chapter 19

The Final Night

The directions were written out, but somehow after passing McGuire Air Force Base on the way to Browns Mills, New Jersey, Regina found herself on a four-lane highway going the wrong way. She was alone with Arlena; Ernest was at home with the other children. It was Sunday morning and there wasn't much traffic, so she craned her neck around and drove the car backward for half a mile. Finally they got back on the right road. It was one of those strange twists of fate that she would always regret.

"If I had just kept going and gotten lost," she's thought a thousand times since then, "by the time we finally got to the hospital maybe it would have been too late to do the operation, and if they had rescheduled it and done it another day, maybe Arlena would still be alive."

That night in the hospital, after all the tests were done, Arlena still seemed vibrant and vivacious. A baby was in the room across the hall. Arlena loved babies and she played with it while Regina went down to the cafeteria to get something to eat. By the time she came back, Arlena was back in her room in the bed by herself. Fear had taken over again.

With her little shoulders hunched and her chin against her chest, she said, "Oh, Mommy, I was so scared without you here."

"Honey," Regina answered, gathering the trembling child up in her arms and trying to calm her. "I'm here, I'm here. I'll stay with you every second. I'll stay with you forever."

Slowly the shivering stopped, and Arlena asked for the Bible. Regina read her a passage or two, then Arlena began to read. She fell asleep holding the Bible with one hand and her mother with the other.

Chapter 20

Never Say Goodbye

The surgery was a success. When Arlena opened her eyes, Regina was right there holding on to her hand, just as she had promised. Irisa was there too. For the first time in Arlena's life her skin was rosy, not blue. Even her lips were pink.

"It's all over," Regina whispered ecstatically. "And you look just beautiful. All the boys will fall in love with you."

Arlena was still too weak to talk, but her eyes were glowing with astonished delight. Regina bent over and kissed her forehead.

"You made it," she said.

"I made it," Arlena repeated, with her voice so light and soft it was almost a thought.

"Look, honey," Irisa said, pointing to a ring Arlena had taken off just before the surgery. "I'm wearing your ring for you until you come home."

"I love you," Arlena whispered.

———

Toward evening everything began to change. Arlena experienced pain. She had not had any medication for hours because the doctors wanted the anesthetic to wear off completely.

The nurse began putting medication into an artery in Arlena's neck. Arlena winced and moved back in the bed. "Arlena," the nurse hissed, taking her by the arm and bearing down, "if you move, I'll stick you." Arlena stayed still, but the nurse had already decided to strap her hands to the bed. She held her tightly as she strapped the buckles.

The fluid in Arlena's lungs began to build up. She tried hard to swallow and to talk, but she had a breathing tube in her throat. She moved her hands and fingers frantically. Suddenly a look of terror entered her eyes, then they became glazed. She turned her head to the side and closed her eyes.

"Something's wrong," Regina gasped. "Oh my God. She's not breathing."

"You're going to have to leave," the nurse snapped. "You're upsetting her."

The nurse called the doctor in. Arlena's heart had stopped. He revived her. She weakened again, and finally after another attempt to revive her failed, the doctor said she was in a coma and had only a few hours left to live.

Irisa, who had been talking to the doctor, walked into the waiting room with a terrible sense of fear. The first thing she saw was her father crying in the rocking chair. She was almost twenty, but she had never seen him cry before. "Damn," she heard him sob as he slammed his fist into the rocking chair. "God, don't take another of my babies." Irisa ran to him and hugged him. He looked at her with a blank stare. Regina was crying too and pacing frantically.

"Pray for my daughter; she's dying. Oh pray for my daughter," she said as two strangers walked through the waiting room. Then the doctor called them all back in. Ernest stood at the foot of the bed, his eyes riveted on the monitor, constantly watching it. He couldn't take his eyes off the monitor. Suddenly there was a beeping sound, then everything stopped. Ernest stood transfixed, counting down the numbers as Arlena's pulse dropped.

"She's gone," the nurse said.

"But I promised her she wouldn't die. I promised her she wouldn't die," Irisa gasped, rocking as she spoke, then falling.

"She fainted," the doctor called, catching her and lifting her into a wheelchair.

At first Regina stood absolutely still. There was Arlena, only nine years old and so beautiful, with her cheeks and lips finally the color of rose petals. Then Regina began to sway from side to side like a damaged wall leaning inward. She wanted to cry out, but she struggled to keep her mouth closed and the screams locked inside. At least those were still hers. Images of Vivia flooded into her consciousness. This had all happened before, thirteen years ago to the day. The pain was familiar but it was worse. She had had Vivia for only six weeks before she lost her. This was different. This was Arlena, Arlena, Arlena. She tried to move toward Arlena, but her legs felt overwhelmingly heavy. She wanted this death to envelop her and suck her into a bottomless grave beside Arlena. At the same time she was filled with panic. Panic that moved from her ankles up through her spinal column to the back of her neck and then into her head, where it stayed along with the drumbeat that was really the beat of Arlena's heart or her own, she couldn't tell which.

Through the haze she could see that somehow Irisa had lifted herself out of the wheelchair and was kneeling beside Arlena, kissing her face and stroking her beautiful hair.

"Her hair, her hair," Irisa was crying softly. "Can I have some of her hair?"

Regina clenched her teeth and bit down on her tongue, but her mouth began to pull open again. Suddenly her scream pierced the air and tore through the room. "Oh my God, my baby, my baby! God took my baby!" she cried.

Chapter 21

The Funeral

When Ernest pulled up to the funeral parlor, Regina opened the car door and fell out, right into the gutter. She didn't even try to get up. Ernest felt the fear in the pit of his belly as he raced around to grab her. Her large, empty eyes fixed on his face as he lifted her. He saw her dazed expression and behind it the wild grief.

Regina could smell the cut flowers and see her sister's hair blowing in the breeze, just as Arlena's had. People were everywhere, greeting each other, whispering, crying, hugging. Their lives were still going on. She closed her eyes for a minute and took a deep breath. When she opened them, she saw Irisa bent over the casket, stroking Arlena's hair again and caressing her fingers.

"Daddy, it's blood. She's bleeding," Irisa shrieked, suddenly recoiling in fear.

"It's just embalming fluid, honey," Ernest whispered. Concerned relatives began trying to pull Irisa away from the coffin.

"No," Irisa said, her voice rising like a clear flame in the darkness. "Don't take me away. She's my sister. It's the last few minutes we have together."

Regina stood watching. "Let her grieve in her own way," she said, finding the strength from somewhere to gently embrace Irisa.

The others were already starting to leave for the cemetery. Little Barry was skipping around their feet singing, "She's with Jesus now. She's with Jesus now."

The next time they gathered, the casket was lowered into the ground. Ernest's brother August was presiding, saying something about how fragile and precious Arlena was and what a loving spirit she had. For a minute Regina could hear him. "Her sweetness and the joy she brought us was immeasurable. We are all asking God why this little girl had to die. We are asking with our hearts and there is no good answer and no understanding. We struggle through the grief of this separation and have no answer." Then Regina's eyes shifted to the coffin and the cold, damp, newly shoveled brown earth. She saw the small stones and blades of grass. "Oh, God, who will care for Arlena now and give her medicine and keep her warm?"

"Regina," Ernest whispered, reaching for her hand, shaking it, trying to bring her back. She looked up and seemed to gaze languidly at him from the very center of her soul. Then her face glazed over, her hand slipped away, and Ernest knew he had lost her again to the soft, gentle glow above the coffin.

Part IV

BLOOD BOND

There is no
erasing this;
The central
memory
of what we are
to one
another . . .
You shall be a
child of the
mother
As of old, and
your face will not
be turned from
me.

R O B I N   M O R G A N

Chapter 22

The Lawsuit

Two weeks after Arlena's death, Marvin Ellin, a sixty-five-year-old, media-savvy malpractice lawyer from Baltimore, filed a one-hundred-million-dollar lawsuit in Tampa Federal Court against Hardee Memorial Hospital.

Ellin called the baby swap "tantamount to kidnapping." He was convinced that it was deliberate. Just looking at it, he said he could tell that the birth certificate was altered. Besides, the scientific evidence was more than 99.9 percent positive. Doctors at Johns Hopkins said that it was virtually impossible that the Twiggs with their O-group blood could have produced this B-positive child.

"It is one of the strangest cases in medical history," the *Washington Post* wrote in the largest type used since the Baby M case. The *Miami Herald* stated: "The Pennsylvania couple is alleging gross negligence and fraud on the part of old Dr. William Black, distinguished Dr. Ernest Palmer, the man who takes the kids' tonsils out, gray-haired nurse Dena Spieth and Dr. Adley Sedaros, the pediatrician who built the nice new house."

"It's simply bizarre," said Harrell Connelly, the new administrator of Hardee Memorial Hospital and the fifth defendant in the suit. "But we're taking it very seriously. It's just so hard to believe that this could happen at such a small hospital, and it's totally unbelievable that it could happen deliberately."

The doctors, nurses and aides who worked at Hardee Memorial Hospital when Regina Twigg's baby was born claimed from the start that no one remembered anything. The only record at the county courthouse involving anyone from the hospital at that time was a thick lawsuit filed against Dr. Adley Sedaros in 1978, the same year that Regina Twigg and Barbara Coker Mays had given birth. Eight construction companies had sued the physician for failing to pay more than twenty thousand dollars he owed them for work on his new house. He reached a settlement with them and then moved quietly away.

William Black, the baby doctor, had also left town five years earlier, causing Hardee Memorial to close its delivery room. A secretary who answered his phone in Ocean Springs, Mississippi, told reporters he was out of town for the weekend and couldn't be reached.

Ernest Palmer, who was reached at Hardee Memorial Hospital, where he still practiced medicine, said, "I certainly wouldn't switch babies on anyone, but I guess we can be sued by anyone."

Dena Spieth, who had retired, refused on the advice of hospital attorneys to say anything at all except "I'm drawing a complete blank on the 1978 births."

But the media didn't go away. In fact, journalists from as far away as Australia and Japan were giving major coverage to the case. It was every parent's nightmare and it clearly had worldwide appeal.

On Friday, September 9, Dr. Black called his office from

Grand Rapids, Michigan, where he had gone to visit his mother-in-law. As soon as his nurse, Ann Findelisen, answered, Black could hear the tension in her voice. "What's going on?" he said.

"Oh my God. You haven't heard. You're plastered all over the front page of the Florida newspapers. Someone is suing you for one hundred million. The phone's been ringing constantly. The newspapers, television stations, wire services and magazines from all over the country keep calling. Do you remember the names Dr. Palmer, Dr. Sedaros and Regina Twigg? She says her baby was switched or sold nine and a half years ago."

Dr. Black returned home to find articles in every newspaper and a pile of messages on his answering machine. Some were from patients canceling their appointments; others were from old friends who said they were praying for him. He called his lawyer, Billy Brown, and said, "I just decided I want to give an interview to the Biloxi *Sun/Daily Herald* and WLOX. I want to do them together so there can't be any misunderstanding and so I make it clear that this is the only interview I'm going to do until I have more information. My patients deserve a speedy response and this is the only way I can think of to do it."

"You're taking a terrible chance," the lawyer told him. "But if you're going to do it, keep it short and general. We have no specifics to discuss. I don't think I should be there. It might look too defensive when there's nothing to defend. All you did was deliver a baby."

Black called the paper and the TV station and arranged to meet reporters at the *Sun/Daily Herald*'s office. He talked for a long time, but all he told them was that he really didn't know what had happened. He said that the Twiggs had his sincere sympathy. They showed about ninety seconds of the interview on TV.

When he got back to the office he found some certified documents from Marvin Ellin. Black brought them over to his lawyer and sat there while Billy Brown read them. After what seemed like forever, Billy looked up. "Don't worry," he said. "They're charging medical negligence and fraud without any specifics. The complaint was put together in one hell of a hurry. . . . The girl died on August 23, the suit was filed on September 7." Brown pointed out that the lawyer didn't give the ninety-days' notice that Florida law demands before releasing it to the press. He also wondered if Arlena's blood was ever typed during one of the earlier hospitalizations. "If so," he said, "that's when discovery began, and they may be past the statute of limitations. Her lawyers were in such a rush to file they may have failed to check on that."

Black still didn't feel reassured. "I think I'm getting paranoid," he confided. He had begun to hear noises on his home telephone and kept getting wrong numbers when he used his automatic dialing system. "I can't help thinking that a wiretap might be messing up my line."

"I doubt it," Billy said. Just the same, about that time Black began noticing a truck that didn't belong to anyone in the neighborhood cruising past his house pretty regularly. It was driven by a man with binoculars.

Billy Brown called again the next day. "I just got a call from a reporter in St. Petersburg asking if you've ever heard the name Barbara Mays. Ring any bells?"

"No," Black said. But after he hung up he found her chart in a box filled with old office records. He put it beside Regina Twigg's chart and compared the two. He called Brown back. "I vaguely remember the deliveries. I've been studying the charts. There are some things about them that trouble me." He told Brown that according to the charts the Twigg baby was cared for by Adley Sedaros. But for some reason Ernest Palmer had made every entry on them except for one—the critical one, the heart defect diagnosis. All Palmer's entries indicated that the Twigg baby was normal. Then on December 5, just before discharge, Sedaros examined her and apparently recorded that the heart murmur was discovered. The chart said he ordered a chest x-ray, a cardiogram and blood gas testing. Palmer then canceled the order for the blood gas testing, which would have revealed the baby's blood type. Another strange thing Black noticed was that Palmer, not Sedaros, told the Twiggs that their baby was abnormal. Palmer also discharged the baby and set up an appointment with the Twiggs in his office.

Since the babies were delivered three days apart, Black knew the bands couldn't have been put on the wrong babies by accident. The cord blood samples couldn't have been accidentally mislabeled for the same reason. Most babies lose weight between the time they are delivered and the time they are discharged, so Black thought it was possible that one identifying band could slip off. But the idea that all four bands had slipped off both babies' wrists and ankles at the same time stretched credulity.

Early in October, five weeks after making the case world famous, Marvin Ellin dropped it. Billy Brown figured it was because he hadn't known about an earlier blood typing. Brown was right. Regina hadn't even told Ernest. She was embarrassed to admit she had kept it a secret for so long, especially from her own husband. It had never even occurred to her that the lawyer would say that she had waited too long and the statute of limitations had passed.

When Black heard the news he was relieved, but what really delighted him was that John Blakely, the Twiggs' new lawyer, was dropping all the criminal charges and refiling the case as a malpractice suit against the hospital. Thank God he and all the other doctors were off the hook.

The Voice of Regina Twigg

I think I've relived her death a thousand times, but her funeral I just blocked out. It was like a dream to me. I needed to say goodbye to her again to try to make it real. I also wanted to give those who couldn't come to the funeral a chance to pay their respects.

Pastor Max, a preacher from the Langhorne United Methodist Church, heard about our situation and offered to let us have a memorial service the week after the funeral. He officiated at it. After the service, Pastor Max would sometimes stop by the house and give us all a big hug and words of encouragement, just to let us know that he loved us and cared about us.

I said, "Pastor Max, I'm sorry I can't sit through your church services, but I get too upset."

"Regina," he said. "You're not here to support me. I'm here to support you."

I remember one time I went over to his church. It was eight months after she died, and I thought, well, maybe I'll attend a sing-along, but I had to get up and go outside because I saw a little girl in a nearby pew who reminded me of Arlena and I started to cry and cry. Pastor Max came out. He followed me out. He gave me a great big bear hug and held on to me for the longest time. He just stood there and held on to me.

I didn't go out of the house for six months after Arlena's death. I didn't even walk to the grocery store down the street. I didn't drive a car for a year.

When the other children needed me, I tried to be there for them. I really, desperately tried. Ernest used to say, "Regina, we are all these kids have. If we fall apart, what will happen to them?"

From August to January, Barry had been in a state of shock. He was experiencing the loss without understanding the meaning of death. When he went to school his teacher would talk to him and he didn't even know she was talking to him. It was like he was in a daze. He couldn't answer her. We had to take him out of school. There's no way he would have ever made it in kindergarten through that year.

I kept him at home with me. Ernest would get up to get ready for work and he'd bring Barry in and lay him on the bed beside me. I would just put my arm around him. Finally, around January, I put him back in preschool for a couple of days a week.

One day after he was back in school, he sat down on the chair in the dining room, looked at me wistfully and said, "I wish I had chocolate candy and Arlena." He brought home a valentine the first February after she died and said, "I wanted to give this to Arlena, but I'll have to give it to Irisa."

Ernie was twelve and angry. He would say, "If God loved her he could have left her here with us."

He would sit on his bed for hours at a time, rooted to the spot, and he would rock. Then one night after midnight Irisa came downstairs and found him sitting at a desk writing Arlena a letter. It said, "I loved you Arlena, you were sweet, you were beautiful." He was crying.

Irisa, who was nineteen, began to cry too. "I know Ernie," she said. "I know."

It was so hard for all the kids. Gina had been staying at my friend Laura's house while Arlena had her surgery. When Arlena died Laura decided it would be best to tell her.

"Well, how's Arlena?" Gina said. She was smiling, waiting for good news.

"Honey," Laura answered, "Arlena's with the Lord now."

"No, no!" Gina screamed. She fell on the floor, hysterical. Her body went into spasms. Then she became rigid and couldn't move. Laura was just scared to death. It was hours before Gina could walk again without support.

For a long time after that Gina was plagued by nightmares about Arlena, mostly things she wished she had done. Finally she decided that the nightmares were better than nothing because at least they brought Arlena back.

Normia couldn't bear to go to school or face the kids. For weeks she had to be coaxed out of her room. Tommy, who had always been inward, shut everyone out. He just became a part of the walls.

Laura stopped by one day to see how we were doing. Suddenly we heard Irisa sobbing hysterically in the shower. We rushed in. "Why did God do this?" she kept crying. "Why is there such suffering in the world? Why did God allow Arlena to suffer? Why did he take her when she wanted so much to live?" We finally calmed her down. Laura kept trying to answer her questions. I couldn't, because I was still searching for the answers myself.

Irisa also began visiting the grave. She'd take a basket of flowers and sit there talking to Arlena, telling her the events of her life. When Irisa got married and when she became pregnant, she made special trips to the grave to tell Arlena. She sometimes even wanted to sleep on the grave because she felt that on that ground she'd be close to Arlena. They'd be side by side again, like the last night that Arlena slept in her bed.

I was also having a hard time. For eight months I just couldn't bear for anyone to get close to me. I shut my feelings off. I said, "Keep your distance. Let me reach out again, when I can." For eight months Ernest just waited for me to reach out to him again. Finally one night I turned toward him and touched his shoulder. He reached out and took me in his arms. I cried and cried and said, "How do you stop hurting?"

"You don't," he answered gently. "You just keep on living."

Many different times I too would ask God, "Why? Why didn't you let me die instead of her?" I had a terrible feeling of guilt. I kept thinking, "It's my fault. It's my fault. I killed her. I killed her. I didn't make the right decision. She died because of me. She died because of me. If only I had done something different." I thought of this and I thought of that. I thought of a hundred "I should haves."

One day when Ernest came home from work Irisa said, "Dad, Mom really thinks it's her fault and that we all blame her." I think actually it was because I blamed myself so I just expected them to blame me.

Later that day Irisa said she went down into the basement. Her daddy was doing laundry and the tears were just running down his face because he was so worried about me. I couldn't help it if everything reminded me of what I had with that child. The happy times, the difficult times, the image of the lost child is forever in my mind. Her little face, her little ways, her spirit, her mannerisms, her little voice, her everything.

Chapter 23
A New Approach

John Blakely was an experienced trial lawyer. He had been admitted to practice law in all the Florida courts, the U.S. Supreme Court, and the U.S. Court of Appeals. He knew enough about law not to be worried that Regina had known Arlena's blood type for several years. As he saw it, her constant questioning just proved that she never suspected a baby swap. What mother would assume her baby had been switched at birth? Blakely figured the statute of limitations didn't begin until the geneticist at Johns Hopkins actually told the Twiggs that Arlena wasn't their daughter. Besides, Florida had a four-year statute of limitations for claims against hospitals, not a two-year statute, as Marvin Ellin had apparently thought.

What did bother Blakely, though, was a Florida law declaring that state-owned hospitals were entitled to sovereign immunity. That meant Hardee Memorial was not responsible for intentional or criminal acts by its employees. Nothing could be recovered from the hospital by Ellin's one-hundred-million-dollar criminal lawsuit alleging an intentional swap.

On the other hand, if the hospital negligently allowed the swap to occur, there was no established cap on what the hospital would have to pay because it was part of the Florida Patients Compensation Fund.

Negligence was definitely the way to go. The Twiggs had no money, so Blakely agreed to handle the whole thing on a contingency basis. He had an instinct for the big ones and he was rarely wrong.

When Blakely started his Clearwater firm, he often took the cases that other lawyers tossed aside. Now, sixteen years later, his law firm had the largest practice in Pinellas County. Twenty-six other lawyers had joined him. He had offices in Clearwater, Port Richey and Tampa. The practice had stretched to a hundred employees, including secretaries, paralegals and law clerks.

The lanky, boyish, silver-haired lawyer was still disarmingly laid back. He had come a long way from the days when he had no clients, one secretary, a card table, a telephone and a tiny office next door to an X-rated movie theater. Blakely was sharp and creative. He personally chose the five-acre site on Chestnut Street that housed the new Clearwater offices and designed the rambling gray wood buildings. Blakely didn't take small cases anymore. Just the same, each lawyer in the firm still provided at least ten hours of free legal service a year to help the poor.

The first thing he did when he took the Twiggs on was to dismiss Ellin's lawsuit and give the hospital six months' notice as Florida law required. After that he clamped a gag order on the Twiggs. It was time to quiet things down and try to figure out what had really happened at Hardee Memorial Hospital ten years earlier.

Chapter 24

Hardee County, Florida

Back in December of 1978, the road to Hardee Memorial Hospital was a country road, strewn with bushy palmetto plants with green leaves that branched out from trunks and dotted the barren roadway like stunted palm trees. Bleached white sand, scrub grass and lantana leaves hid rabbits, raccoons, opossums and armadillos. The barbed-wire fences and tiny man-made lakes were the only signs of human influence to be seen among the scrub brush, where cattle grazed by day among the rattlesnakes.

When they crossed the concrete bridge over Charlie Creek and finally entered the main street of Wauchula, it was deserted except for a couple of ranchers walking around in their riding clothes.

They were the cattlemen critical to the farming economy of this little central Florida town. Some sixty-five thousand head of cattle made Hardee County one of America's leading livestock centers. But the greatest resource of the area was citrus. Fifty thousand acres of orange groves produced everything from seedlings to orange juice. Still, this was a small town with small-town values. The people who'd lived here all their lives claimed that everyone who mattered was related to everyone else. They all belonged to the same clubs and the same churches. Some of the cowboys were also politicians, and a handful of them, along with a few prominent founding families, ran this town. Among them were the Cokers.

In the 1920s, Bryant Coker set up the first funeral home in the city. It provided twenty-four-hour-a-day service. Coker became rich and powerful. He was also sensitive and smart. He took care of people when they were vulnerable, and everyone was indebted to him.

Scarcely a person in Hardee County hadn't been touched by Bryant Coker and scarcely a person wasn't grateful. All of the Coker family were entrepreneurs. They played such an important role in everything, from tax assessment and elections to ranching and funeral parlors, that without them, some people said, the area would never have grown as it did. They even had a railroad stop named after them. When it came time to build the fifty-bed modern Hardee Memorial Hospital, Bryant Coker and a few others helped fund the project.

Regina Twigg didn't know anything about the Cokers. She didn't know that Barbara Coker Mays had just delivered the only other white baby in the hospital or that the baby was very sick. Only years later, with the help of two private investigators, did an image of the community, the Cokers and Hardee Memorial Hospital begin to emerge. Vera Polly Rhodes, an aide who worked the night shift from 1976 to 1980, was the first hospital worker to be interviewed by Special Agent Ray Starr, a private investigator in Arcadia, Florida, who ran a corporate investigative and research service.

Rhodes, whose supervisor had once called her "one of the most valuable nursery workers," had a reputation for becoming almost painfully involved with her little patients. Some nurses said she was so good that she spoiled the babies. One accused her of running a fever every time the babies did.

According to Rhodes, babies were sometimes confused. Rhodes remembered a night at about the time that the Twigg baby was born when she came on duty and was told that all the babies were sick. There were six children in the nursery that night. When she went to the crib of the little girl who was crying the loudest and began to change her diaper, she said, "Oh my goodness, you're a little boy." The baby was in the wrong crib. All six babies were in the wrong cribs. They were all sick because they all had each other's bottles.

Rhodes said it took her and her supervisor much of the night to get things straightened out. First they matched the identification bracelets on the babies' wrists and ankles with the names on the cribs. Then they resterilized all the bottles and other equipment.

According to the sworn statement Polly Rhodes gave to Starr, another aide, who usually worked the three to eleven P.M. shift, had stayed on all night shortly before the babies were switched. According to Rhodes, on December 4, the first Monday of December 1978, when she reported for her eleven P.M. to seven A.M. shift, the supervisor on duty stopped her before she could enter the maternity ward and sent her home.

"After news of the switch broke in the media," Rhodes says, someone on the hospital staff "came to my house, very agitated. I was warned not to talk about the incident. 'Polly, you better not say anything. Just tell them you don't want to talk and you're not going to talk and don't.' "

Ray Starr was still searching for more information. There was usually someone who broke down under stress.

In March 1989 he got the tip he'd been waiting for from the local police department. Kathryn Drevermann, a night shift employee at the Avon Park Circle K, was claiming she'd heard a confession. Starr knocked on her door and intro-

duced himself. "I'd like to talk to you about a baby swap," he
said, taking out his identification. "May I come in?"

"Yes sir, you can," she said. "I love babies and if it was me
I'd want my baby back. I'm happy to help any way I can."

"Mrs. Drevermann," Starr said, adjusting the level on his
tape recorder. "From August 1988 to late January 1989, where
were you employed?"

"At Circle K," she answered.

"Circle K, is that a fast-food store?"

"Yes sir, a convenience store."

"You had a customer come in, about a month ago. Would
you tell me about that customer?"

"Yes sir, she was the only customer there. She came in and
she wanted a pack of cigarettes. It was an off brand, one I had
to get down on the floor and dig for. She was having trouble
breathing."

Detective Starr: "Did she specify a brand?"

Mrs. Drevermann: "Yes sir, but I don't remember if it was
Carleton or some other brand that I don't usually have on the
shelf. She said she had been sick and she wasn't supposed to
be driving a car but she had to have a cigarette."

Detective Starr: "How was she dressed that night,
ma'am?"

Mrs. Drevermann: "She was in her gown and her house
shoes."

Detective Starr: "What time would that have been?"

Mrs. Drevermann: "It had to be around eleven-thirty or
maybe near twelve o'clock."

Detective Starr: "How do you place the time?"

Mrs. Drevermann: "By the cleaning."

Detective Starr: "You start cleaning when the customers
stop coming in?"

Mrs. Drevermann: "Yes sir."

Detective Starr: "Can you describe this lady?"

Mrs. Drevermann: "She had dark hair. She was between five foot three and five foot four. She was about a hundred and twenty pounds."

Detective Starr: "You say her hair was dark?"

Mrs. Drevermann: "Yes sir, it was dark hair. It was dark enough to be considered black or real dark brown."

Detective Starr: "Did she appear to be in good mental health, but nervous maybe?"

Mrs. Drevermann: "Yes sir, she seemed like she just wanted to rattle on, real nervous like."

Detective Starr: "Did she impress you as being a mental case?"

Mrs. Drevermann: "Seemed like more nervous or restless."

Detective Starr: "Did she seem to be on medication?"

Mrs. Drevermann: "Yes sir, it was prescription drugs. She pulled one out while she was talking to me and I glanced at it."

Detective Starr: "Okay. After she purchased her cigarettes, she started smoking. How was she smoking her cigarettes?"

Mrs. Drevermann: "Chain-smoking."

Detective Starr: "What was the conversation? I understand she talked to you for about an hour."

Mrs. Drevermann: "Yes sir, she was just talking. Then somehow she brought up the subject of the baby switch."

Detective Starr: "You're talking about the Twigg and Mays babies. Would that be correct?"

Mrs. Drevermann: "Yes sir."

Detective Starr: "All right, and what did she say then?"

Mrs. Drevermann: "She said that, ah, she was just talking about them being swapped and all and she thought they ought to just leave well enough alone. She said if they had been swapped, they ought to be left alone. She said something about an investigation that was going on and she had been called in. Then she said she had been ordered to switch those babies' bands one to the other."

Detective Starr: "In other words, switch the Mayses' baby's band to the Twiggs' baby, that's what she meant?"

Mrs. Drevermann: "Yes sir."

Detective Starr: "Did she say anything else?"

Mrs. Drevermann: "She said that money was involved but she didn't know how it had changed hands or how much money was involved."

Detective Starr: "She didn't seem to be a mental case like a walkaway from a mental hospital, did she?"

Mrs. Drevermann: "No sir, she just seemed like she wanted somebody to talk to. When she smoked the cigarettes she seemed like she was gasping for air, she coughed. Her voice sounded like she was choked up, trying to get up some phlegm or something. I had put an ashtray up on top of the counter because it wasn't busy and I figured she was there to talk for a while."

Detective Starr: "Okay. Did she mention the names of any doctors?"

Mrs. Drevermann: "Yes sir. She mentioned Palmer and Black a number of times, and one other, but I can't remember the other name. It sounded like the name started with an S. I thought she said Sodority or something like that. She said that Dr. Palmer was a pretty good doctor and if he had ordered it they ought to just leave it alone."

Detective Starr: "I know you're not a psychologist, ma'am, but did it seem like she might have been suffering from a conscience problem?"

Mrs. Drevermann: "It seems like it, because she just kept saying they ought to leave well enough alone."

Detective Starr: "Would you recognize this lady again if you saw her?"

Mrs. Drevermann: "Yes sir."

Detective Starr: "Did she say anything about where she lived?"

Mrs. Drevermann: "She said something about not living

very far from the store. She said she should not be out dressed the way she was but she had to have a pack of cigarettes and she didn't live very far from the store."

Detective Starr: "Would you raise your right hand? Do you, Kathryn Ann Drevermann, solemnly swear that the information you have given me here on this day is true to the best of your knowledge?"

Mrs. Drevermann: "Yes sir, I do."

Detective Starr: "Thank you, ma'am."

Kathryn Drevermann later identified the woman as Patsy Webb, a nurse's aide in the hospital nursery. Patsy denies ever speaking to Kathryn Drevermann.

Chapter 25

Going Public

On September 8, 1988, the day that would have been Barbara Coker Mays's fortieth birthday, Velma Coker opened her morning newspaper and read that Ernest and Regina Twigg were suing Hardee Memorial Hospital for one hundred million dollars because their healthy baby was switched with a sick one in December 1978. The article said that only two white babies were born there during that week. Velma picked up her phone. "Bob," she said, "a storm is brewing on the horizon. Read the newspapers."

Actually, the press had already tracked Bob Mays down. The first thing reporters did when he came to his door was promise him they wouldn't use his name or Kimberly's. That won him over right away. He smiled, invited them in and cooperated. All the reporters privately agreed that it was a shame such a nice, friendly guy and his daughter were getting caught up in a mess like this.

Two weeks later Bob decided to go public. He told reporters that he was afraid that if he didn't tell Kimberly himself she might find out from somebody else. "I'm just tired of living a lie here and trying to hide her from the press and worrying about who might confront my daughter at school or on the way home." Then he held a news conference to tell the world who he and his daughter were and to say he would fight "to the ends of the earth" to keep Kimberly, even if a genetic test showed he was not her father.

"I wouldn't care if they traced her to Cabbage Patch, USA," he said. "I'm her father. She resembles her mother and aunt. She looks like them, she acts like them. You know—her mannerisms, certain poses, certain ways she moves herself and her legs. She has her mother's legs." He smiled. "Her mother had a very unusual pair of legs."

When Bob scheduled the conference he had agreed to talk but not to be identified by name. Even that limited promise brought a mob of reporters from all over the country. Before Bob arrived, two TV crews had an all-out shouting match over whose lights should go where in the crowded conference room. It got so bad it looked like they were going to start punching each other. When Bob finally began to speak, the TV crews quieted down, but the reporters went wild shouting for him to talk into the cluster of microphones. His voice shook when he began talking; then it strengthened.

"When I first heard the Twiggs wanted my daughter, I thought it was a terrible joke. I couldn't believe this was really happening to me. Initially, I thought I could keep Kimberly from finding out about the furor closing in. But it became increasingly difficult. There were phone calls late at night and knocks on the door when reporters came to question me. Kimberly had begun to wonder why she couldn't go out and play like she used to." Then Bob told the crowd that he had finally decided to tell her everything. "I picked Kimberly up from school one day," he said. "I bought her some bubble-gum-flavored frozen yogurt and sat her down on the veranda to talk. I'm the same guy that had to sit down and tell her that her real mother had died, okay? And then I had to explain how my second wife and I were divorcing. The one certainty that goes straight through all these episodes is that in the final analysis Daddy was always there. We've been through death, we've been through divorce, and in every case we came through together. The only rise I got out of her was when she thought perhaps she might have to go and be someone else's daughter. When I promised her she would not, she calmed down. She was a real trouper."

As Bob explained it, Kimberly's only concern was that she might be separated from him. Otherwise, he said, Kimberly was pleased about the attention. "It's something new and exciting. I think she's going to have a little fun with this." He called Kimberly a ham who loved being the center of attention and got A's and B's in school.

Bob paused and looked out at the sea of reporters. It was like a movie. "As for me, I've gone through the full range of emotions from fear and concern to humor," he said. "Right now I really don't know how I feel about it." After thanking reporters and giving them the impression that he was about as close as any man could get to being the ideal father, Bob added that he and Kimberly led a typical Florida life-style and often went boating and even skiing in Vail, Colorado, one of Kimberly's favorite places.

That night, after reading the press report, Cindy couldn't help herself. She forgot all of her resolve. Something, maybe the memory of Vail, made her pick up the telephone and call Bob. "Oh, Bob, I'm so sorry," she said. "Is there anything I can do to help?" At that moment she might even have jumped into her car and driven to Sarasota—that was how overwhelmed she felt.

"Thanks kid," he said, "but I'm a big boy. I can manage." Then he hung up.

The next morning at school, every kid in the class gathered around Kimberly. She sat at her desk, amazed and smiling.

"We all know that Kimberly's getting a lot of attention

right now," the teacher said when she came into the classroom. "But please, as her friends, let's not dwell on this or treat Kimberly any differently today than we did yesterday."

Meanwhile, Arthur Ginsberg, one of the best-known divorce lawyers in Sarasota, had decided to help Bob fight for Kimberly. "It's an exciting case," he said. "And God knows how much more bizarre it's going to get." Then the short, gray-haired attorney, who was built like a fireplug, added, "Personally, I just want it to be over with and for Kimberly to stay with her dad." Ginsberg, who had used well-known experts in many of his divorce cases, quickly began introducing testimony in court. Two of the experts he hired, Dr. Albert J. Solnit, a Yale University professor of pediatrics and psychiatry and Dr. Joseph Goldstein, a professor at Yale Law School and Yale University Child Study Center, agreed that Kimberly's mental health and stability would be harmed even by a genetic test.

Goldstein, who had studied the separation of Jewish children from their families during the Holocaust, wrote, "If you were a child of ten, would you understand why you would have to lose your loving parents because of some adult notion of the law?"

Dr. Lee Salk, a professor of psychiatry and pediatrics at New York Hospital/Cornell Medical Center, had also been hired. "Kimberly should not be made to fear the possibility of losing her father," he said. "If there is truly any concern and love for this child on the part of Mr. and Mrs. Twigg, they will find it in their hearts to leave her alone and let her get on with her life."

Once the momentum in Bob's favor started growing, it kept increasing like a big snowball rolling down a hill. "If you really love a child you don't risk coming in and traumatizing the child because of some biological claim," said Dr. William Hafling, a St. Petersburg psychologist. Soon lawyers joined psychiatrists, and the public clamor grew.

"The law assumes that biological parents are the best custodians," added Cynthia Green, chairman elect of the Florida Bars Family Law Section. "*But* it also says that a child should not be placed with parents who are unfit. If it would harm the child to be taken from Bob Mays, if it would cause the most severe psychological trauma, then by definition the Twiggs would be unfit."

The image of a lonely single parent increased public sympathy. According to the *St. Petersburg Times*, Barbara's death devastated Mays. Bob himself added, "The only thing that kept me going was the thought that I did have Kimberly. I had to do something to get back on my feet because I had a life there that I was responsible for."

Judge Andy Owens, who was assigned to preside over the unprecedented case, had been dubbed "Solomon of Sarasota" because people thought his role was so difficult.

Journalists and spectators whispered nervously, then fell silent when the six-foot-six-inch former basketball player from the University of Florida walked into the courtroom on December 2, 1988. He wore a black robe instead of an orange and blue uniform and was greeted by reverence instead of a roaring crowd, but people still thought of him as a star. "Good morning, Judge," the lawyer said. Owens nodded and smiled.

The all-American hero of two decades ago had kept his reputation for staying calm in tough situations. "I have to make a Solomon-like decision without Solomon's ability to make those kinds of decisions," Owens told reporters before entering the courtroom. "So I'm tapping on the discipline I learned as an athlete. Just as I ignored the fans when shooting baskets, now I have to screen out the emotions and the legal theatrics surrounding the strangest dispute since Baby M. You've got to block out a lot of things to get to the real issue, the heart of it," he explained.

Owens had always been independent and good at what he

did. While still a teenager at Hillsborough High School in Seminole Heights, a suburb of Tampa, he had established himself as the string-bean sensation of the basketball team. Fifty-five colleges and universities sought him out and offered him scholarships. As an undergraduate finance major at the University of Florida, he had one of the highest academic averages of any college ballplayer. After graduation he accepted another academic scholarship and enrolled in law school at the University of Florida. In law school, Owens was often seen driving a Triumph, riding a 650 motorcycle and socializing. For a while his grades dropped, but he buckled down and graduated in the top third of the class. In 1983, he was appointed to a two-year term as a Sarasota circuit judge. In 1985 he was reappointed to a six-year term. He became known as a good judge, very bright, very independent, very funny and sometimes a bit irreverent. But Owens was approaching this case with the utmost seriousness. "I'll have to listen carefully to legal arguments and try to make this decision based on what will be best for Kimberly," he said.

On December 2, 1988, Owens listened intently as Ginsberg tried to head off a genetic test for Kimberly. "She does not want to meet the Twiggs. She does not want to have the blood taken from her. She does not want genetic testing. She wants to be left alone. My client doesn't care whose child she is; he just wants to be allowed to continue to raise her."

When Owens seemed unmoved Ginsberg suggested a meeting between the Twiggs and Bob Mays, neither of whom attended the hearing, so "the Twiggs could see what a decent and honorable, wonderful father he is."

John Blakely stood up. "My clients will be happy to meet with Mr. Mays," he said, "when he admits that Kimberly is in fact the child of Mr. and Mrs. Twigg."

"Hold it," Ginsberg interrupted. "I'm asking right now, what do they intend to do if they can prove Kimberly is their child?"

"The Twiggs would not have to do anything," Blakely answered calmly. "Since even before there were laws, the right of the natural parents to raise their child was recognized. My understanding of the law is that if my clients are the natural parents they don't have to ask the court for custody. Mr. Mays will have the burden of going forward to seek custody, not us."

Ginsberg requested that the case be dismissed. Owens rejected the request and authorized Blakely to take a few critical depositions from the doctors and nurses who worked at Hardee Memorial Hospital. Then he shook his head, and with a troubled look he said, as if to himself, "Solomon had to consider it, but no one else that I'm aware of."

In an impromptu interview with reporters outside the courtroom, Blakely explained his clients' position. "Of course, the Twiggs will investigate very thoroughly what would be best for the child and what changes if any should be made. I've just obtained hospital medical records that prove that the baby Barbara Coker Mays had given birth to was weak, had poor circulation, blue extremities and type B blood, just like Arlena's. I'll be returning to court to seek an order for genetic testing based on these records and the depositions I'm going to take."

The next morning Bob Mays called his own impromptu press conference. "I don't recall my baby girl having bluish skin," he drawled, "and I'm sure I would have remembered if anyone said she had a bluish tint. I believe Mrs. Twigg coined the phrase 'You don't turn love on and off like a faucet.' This child is mine; whether she's genetically mine or biologically mine, that isn't the issue. The only issue is what's best for Kimberly. I can't see that being anything other than what Kimberly and I have together right now. As a parent I find it highly offensive that these people continue to pursue this. We've got six of the best people in the world saying "Don't do this . . . stop. How much more do we have to hurt this child before we stop?" He paused, his face flushed with anger, but he was not out of control. "I want the Twiggs to leave Kimberly alone. She can't understand why someone would be doing something like this to her."

After the press conference Bob confided to a few reporters that nighttime was the worst time for him. "During the day," he explained, "there is little time for fear. Kimberly has homework to do, her bike to ride and fake fingernails to fuss over. I have work. But it is a flexible schedule," he added. "That allows me to spend a lot of time with Kimberly, cooking, boating and helping her with her homework.

"But at night," Bob said, "after Kimberly is in bed, often I can't sleep. I think about the way she bounces through the door every day after school and chirps a familiar greeting. If she's taken away from me," he told the *St. Petersburg Times*, "things like that will kill me. At two o'clock in the afternoon for the rest of my life, I'll hear her say, 'Daddy, I'm home.'"

Chapter 26

Gathering the Evidence

Private investigator Ray Starr had been casing Orchid Lakes, a ten-acre condominium complex, for most of the day. He had checked out the decked swimming pool and tree-filled picnic area. Not a bad place for the money, he concluded. The sale price usually ran around $79,000 with a maintenance fee of $104 per month.

Starr drove around to the west and parked near unit 104, where Robert Mays and his new girlfriend, Darlena Sousa, had been living together since August 1988. Starr's quick check revealed that she was a recently divorced, thirty-two-year-old president of a mechanical contracting firm. Starr turned off the engine to wait. He wondered who'd show up first. Probably the woman, he figured.

At around two-fifteen, he saw a little girl about four foot ten, weighing about ninety pounds, with blond hair that hung just below her shoulders. She had walked part of the distance from the bus stop with another child. Now she waved goodbye, took a key out of her school bag and let herself into unit 104. At five-thirty she came out again, climbed onto a pink bike and rode alone to the Zayre Shopping Center. At about six o'clock she left a Kash and Karry supermarket, carrying a small paper bag. Then she rode home again, took out her key and let herself in. She looked kind of lonely to Starr. At six-thirty Robert Mays had still not come home.

Chapter 27
Cindy's Struggle

Cindy hadn't been feeling well ever since she read the lead editorial in the *Orlando Sentinel*. "Let there be no more talk of genetic tests, lest Kimberly be further traumatized. From birth Kimberly, an only child, has known no other father but Mr. Mays. The affection and trust Mr. Mays and Kimberly share span a decade. Clearly those bonds reveal a true father-daughter relationship, regardless of biology. Kimberly is a human being, not a plant or pet that can be shifted from household to household and expected to adjust. Kimberly Mays deserves to return to the quiet life she has enjoyed with the only father she has ever known."

By the time Cindy finished reading that she was crying. The next day there was another editorial. "Kimberly's mother died of cancer," it said. "And for most of her life she and her father have been a family of two. The sanctity of that family of two and the protection of ten-year-old Kimberly must be paramount in this case. The Twiggs deserve some compensation from Hardee Memorial Hospital for what they have been through, if it is shown that a hospital error robbed them of their child. They don't, however, deserve Kimberly, even if genetic testing shows that she is their biological daughter. Another kind of test would show that Kimberly is the daughter of Robert Mays, the father who for ten years has protected her, housed her, clothed her, taught her and loved her."

"Damn," Cindy said, pouring herself a cup of coffee. She called her father and told him she wanted to talk to the press.

"Now don't be doing that, Cindy," he said. "You know what Dr. Groff told you. You've got no power over this thing. You've got a life to live. Stay out of it; you have Ashlee to take care of. And if anyone contacts you, don't talk to them."

"Don't worry, Daddy," Cindy said, crying again. "Nobody even knows I exist."

Nobody except Bob's lawyer, who called as soon as the case broke. "I understand that you have Kimberly's baby book and some photographs in your possession. We'll be sending someone over tomorrow to pick those things up," he said.

The next day a legal assistant came and asked for the baby book and any other birth records that were in the house. "I'd like to save those things," Cindy said. "They are all I have left of Kimberly."

"Just let me see them," the woman said. Cindy brought out the baby book, and they sat outside on the step looking through it so that Ashlee wouldn't see. The woman flipped through the pages past the list of baby gifts and the page marked "Baby's First Birthday," pausing where it said, "Who were the other mothers you met in the hospital?" Barbara Mays had written, "Mrs. Twigg." Cindy could tell by the woman's expression that Barbara's knowing about Regina and her baby might be significant. But what she really focused on was the tiny armband taped to the front page of the baby book, that and a photograph of the baby that had been taken through the nursery window.

"I don't see why you need that book," Cindy said. "It never meant anything to Bob before."

"I can subpoena it," the woman responded.

"Go ahead," Cindy answered, feeling ornery. She had so little power over the situation these days that she hated to give it up.

"I'll tell you what, Mrs. Mays," the woman said, smiling. "All I really need is the armband and the baby photograph. If you will just let me take those, you can keep the book." Cindy looked at the photograph. "That's funny," she thought. "It really doesn't look like Kimberly." Cindy hesitated. "I'll return it," the woman promised. "I just need it for court, then I'll bring it back."

Cindy felt a dull ache in the back of her head. Maybe it wasn't Kimberly at all, Cindy thought. Maybe it was the other baby. She knew she'd really like to go out somewhere and have a good time, maybe go dancing, and escape from all of this. She tried to think clearly about where it might end if she refused. What difference did it make now anyhow? Suddenly she felt it wasn't worth the hassle. It was Kimberly she wanted, not the baby bracelet, not the photograph. She had a whole box of pictures out in the shed and she couldn't even bring herself to look at them. "You've got it," she answered, trying to push down the raw ache that was rising up inside her. She'd better end this meeting, because in a minute she'd be crying or saying things she shouldn't say.

"Thank you, Mrs. Mays," the legal assistant said. Then, just for a moment, they looked at each other. After that the woman drove away.

The Voice of
Regina Twigg

Most people were afraid to admit they knew me or to come to the house. Occasionally someone who knew us would ask how things were going and give us a supportive word. And there were times when I saw perfect strangers on the street who would say things like, "Are you Mrs. Twigg? You don't owe anybody any apologies. They owe you."

But there were also people who would come up to me and say things like, "Don't upset the child." My comment back to them was, "If somebody took your child and gave it to somebody else without your permission, would you walk away?" After a while I refused to say anything back to them.

Some people said, "Well, you had Arlena for nine and a half years. You should be grateful for that much. You should leave Kimberly alone because you can't replace Arlena with Kimberly." We were very well aware that you can't replace one child with another. We lost Vivia, and we didn't replace Vivia with any other child we had. And we've never, ever expected that we would replace Arlena with Kimberly. There's no child who could ever take the place of Arlena, no matter if I had ten more children given to me.

But there is not another child who could replace Kimberly either. She is our flesh and blood. She is the sister of our children. We want to share in her life and so do her brothers and sisters.

The kids were still having a very hard time. Because now, on top of losing Arlena and dealing with my despair and their own, reporters were looking in our windows and our family was being ridiculed. We were receiving hate mail. The press had turned almost everyone against us. I thought it was natural for us to wonder how this switch had occurred. After all, Bob and Barbara Mays had their baby for four whole days before they got mine. They had a motive, we didn't. When we questioned it the media in Florida turned on us in a persecution rampage. "How dare those Yankee Twiggs from Sebring question this man? How dare they put this Sarasota boy on the defensive? How dare they question him and threaten to snatch his only child out of his arms?" The media thought that we were determined to take custody, not knowing if he was innocent or guilty, not knowing what kind of parent he was. For a long time we backed off the entire custody issue and said, "Let's get the genetic testing done. Then from there, when we have more information, we can make a custodial determination."

But the media in Florida kept writing month after month about how those Twiggs wanted custody and how they were going to snatch poor little Kimberly from the only daddy she had ever known. They made villains of us and a hero of Robert Mays.

Chapter 28

The Photograph

People couldn't understand why anyone would want a little girl who had been calling someone else Daddy for ten years, even if she was theirs. It made them angry and hostile.

Will never had it easy in school. The kids said his head was too large and his eyes didn't focus right. He was a very sweet child, very easygoing, and now that the newspaper reports about the switch were out he was a natural victim. The kids were teasing him about Kimberly, knocking him down on the bus and walking on him. They punched him in the stomach time after time. He came home and beat the table with his fists. "Maybe I'd be better off like Arlena," he said, crying. Regina called the school and spoke to the principal but nothing changed. She called again. "This has to stop," she said. "I don't want to have to go over your head to the administrator or the county office."

After that the principal was very helpful, and so was the teacher. But there was one kid who still kept kicking him. After about a week of it Will turned around and kicked him back hard. The teacher acted like nothing happened. That was it. The teasing and the terrorizing stopped. Things started turning around. Some of the kids told Will they were sorry about what happened to his sister. They wanted to be friends. It helped a lot to have a couple of kids extending kindness to him.

Irisa joined a health club, hoping to work out some of her own frustration and anger, but when the receptionist saw her name on the list she said, "Oh, Twigg. I know who you are," and threw the card at her.

"My God, Mom, everybody acts like we have the plague, like we're someone they're afraid to be around," Normia said. "We hurt too, we're real people too, and we want our sister. Just because there are seven of us doesn't heal our pain. Why do they expect us to think of our sister, our flesh-and-blood sister, as one of the living dead? Our sister's out there somewhere and we're not allowed to know her."

Regina was down. She felt so bad about what the kids were going through she considered dropping the case. Not that she really could have even if she wanted to. "You're not giving up. You're not giving up," all the kids said in unison. "You're going to go on fighting, Mom. Arlena wouldn't want you to give up."

A couple of days after that, every newspaper in the country ran the first picture of Kimberly Mays. She was holding an umbrella and smiling. Ernest and Regina looked at the image of the little girl they had dreamt of so many times and knew instantly that they had found their daughter. In the dreams the face was always unfocused. But now, suddenly, the sight of the child, the actual little girl smiling and wearing Regina's own face, was such a shock that neither of them slept at all that night.

Bob Mays was still telling the press that the Twiggs had no right to meet Kimberly until she was eighteen, even if the blood tests proved that she was their daughter. But now Regina's wavering was gone. She knew she could never give up. In fact, she decided then and there to move back to Florida so they could be closer to Kimberly and get on with the fight.

Part V
FAMILY MATTERS

Standing next
to me in this
lonely crowd
Is a man
who swears he's
not to blame
All day long I
hear him shout
so loud,
Crying out that
he was framed.

BOB DYLAN
"I Shall Be Released"

Chapter 29

Nurses and Doctors

Diana Tinsley Smith, a nurse who was on duty when Regina gave birth, sat at the long white table and glanced nervously over at John Blakely, then at Regina Twigg. "I do remember Barbara," she admitted. "I remember taking care of Barbara."

"I assume over the fourteen-year period that you are a nurse who cared for hundreds if not thousands of people. Isn't that right?" Blakely asked.

"Right, right," Smith answered.

"Then why is it you remember Barbara?"

"Well," she hedged, "I knew her mother and I just knew of Barbara."

"You knew her mother?"

"Uh-huh."

"What is her mother's name?"

"Velma Coker."

"Do you know anything specific? Do you remember anything specific about Barbara Mays's hospitalization?"

"No," Smith said.

"Had you seen her? Had you met her before she came to the hospital to deliver her child in 1978?"

"Yes, I met her previously," Smith acknowledged.

"So you knew that that was her."

"Yes."

Blakely glanced down at his notes, then pointed out that Smith had signed the form stating that Arlena had been given to her proper mother.

"Mr. Blakely, I don't sign a record unless I go through the proper procedure," she said. "My signature there indicated that I took the baby with Ident-a-band 1059 to the mother, Regina Twigg. She received the baby, examined it, determined it was her baby, and I cut the band off in front of her after making sure it was the same corresponding number that she wore. Then I taped one band on the record."

"Okay," Blakely said, moving on to another touchy subject. "On page twelve, under physician's orders, I believe you will see where Dr. Sedaros ordered at eight-thirty in the morning a blood gas test. Did I correctly read that?"

"Yes sir, blood gas is correct," Smith answered.

"Is the next entry below that yours, Mrs. Smith? Is it your handwriting?"

"That's correct."

"Where it says 'omit blood gases,' is that your handwriting?"

"Yes sir."

"And you signed it for Dr. Palmer?"

"That's right," Smith replied. "He gives the verbal order; I write it per his instructions."

"Mrs. Smith," Blakely asked pointedly. "Do you know why the decision was made to omit the blood gas test?"

"I do not know. I don't recall."

"Do you know why he asked you to discharge the baby to his office?"

"No, I don't know. I wrote that upon his order," Smith answered.

"I believe I see your signature down here for the seven A.M. to three P.M. shift on the date December 5, and it looks like you don't have a weight listed for the child on that day."

Smith looked at the record, then back at Blakely. "There's no weight recorded, sir."

"Why not?" he asked. "I mean, can you tell me why you would not have taken the child's weight on that date?"

"No sir, I don't recall," she stammered. "It could have been one of those things that just went by the wayside, you know. It also could have been that possibly the mother and child were, you know, discharged and the weight just wasn't, you know, obtained prior to this recording."

Blakely looked long and hard at her. "You would admit that the child *should* have been weighed and the weight should have been recorded," he said.

"Yes sir," she answered.

Nurse Dena Spieth was next. "How old are you?" John Blakely asked.

She hesitated, then giggled nervously. "I started to say eighty-seven, but I'm sixty-seven. My mother-in-law is eighty-seven. You see I'm having trouble."

Spieth rattled on. She talked about her marriage, her divorce and her children. She even told Blakely that her former mother-in-law was still her best friend.

He smiled sympathetically, then asked her if she could ever recall a time that an identification band had accidentally slipped off a baby's arm.

"As I recall, it happened one time, but not both bands, and we attached it to the foot of the bassinet. I've been racking my brain trying to think and I can only recall that one time."

"Mrs. Spieth, do you know any member of the Mays family?"

"I didn't know that I knew them," Spieth said. "But since then I have discovered that I do know Mrs. Mays's brother, Larry Coker. Before I knew Larry, I knew his wife, Carolyn, who goes to our church."

"All right. How about Regina Twigg? She's sitting here in the room today."

"I know," Dena Spieth said, glancing over at Regina, then looking away.

"Do you recognize her?"

"No, I do not, except for the pictures in the papers."

Blakely turned his attention back to the identification bands. He asked how the clasps were opened.

"They cannot be unclasped in any way. The only way to remove them is to cut them. I can only recall one time," Spieth stammered, "when a very premature baby, it was either the ankle or wrist . . . a premature baby, very tiny. . . . The band slipped off and I can't remember which but not both bands. And we attached it to the foot of the bassinet."

"You did not put it back on the child?" Blakely asked. "You put it on the bassinet?"

"As I recall, because the baby was so small, we were afraid it would slip off again."

"Mrs. Spieth, do you recall the names of any of the aides who worked in the nursery in 1978?" Blakely's voice was soft but the tone was solemn.

"Well, I know there was a Polly Rhodes that worked in the nursery," she said. "I really can't think of anyone else." He let it go at that.

Regina didn't know that Polly Rhodes swore her entrance to the maternity ward on the night of the switch had been blocked. Nor did she know that Rhodes said someone from the hospital had shown up at her house when the case broke and warned her not to talk. What Regina did find extraordinary, however, was something that occurred right after the deposition was over.

Everyone stood up to leave. "Mrs. Twigg," Dena Spieth called out. Regina turned around. "Mrs. Twigg," she repeated, and then suddenly she threw her arms around Regina and began to cry. "Oh, Mrs. Twigg, I'm so sorry," she sobbed, patting Regina on the back. "You're not a bad person. You never deserved this." Then as she straightened up she saw John Blakely's wide-eyed look and the hospital attorney's surprised stare. "Of course you do have all those other children who need you," she stammered, collecting herself. No one, least of all Regina, knew what to make of it.

It was Patsy Webb who provided the first real break in the depositions. The day after Spieth testified, the thin, dark-haired woman with labored breathing admitted that on several occasions identification bands slipped off the babies' wrists or ankles. "We seen them laying wherever they fell," she told Blakely, contradicting Spieth.

"Did you always find the bracelet or anklet in the child's crib, or in other places also? For example, did you ever find an identification bracelet on the floor?"

"The only way it would be on the floor," Webb said, "is if you picked the baby up and it fell off."

"Did that ever happen?" Blakely asked, barely able to hide his excitement.

"Yes, it happened," Webb answered.

"When you went to put the anklet or bracelet back on the child did you have any difficulty in doing it?"

Webb hesitated.

"Was it difficult to slip the band back on or did it slip right back on easily?" Blakely repeated deliberately, keeping his voice as even as he could.

"Not real easy," Webb answered, pausing as if to recollect. "But it slipped back on."

"You slipped it on," Blakely repeated. "You didn't unhook the clasp."

"No," Patsy Webb answered, wheezing slightly. "You couldn't unhook the clasp."

"Did you have to stretch the plastic?"

"Well, if it fell off loosely it could be put back on. She was such a little thing," Webb said, without explaining who "she" was. "We just put it back on and that was it."

"All right, Mrs. Webb. In most instances, when you found a bracelet or anklet had fallen off a newborn child, when you put it back on, did you tighten it?"

"No," she said.

"And when this happened, did you make *any* notation about the incident in the log book?"

"No," she said again. Then Webb told Blakely that she also found babies mixed up and sleeping in the wrong cribs.

"Were the Twigg and Mays babies among those that were mixed up?" Blakely asked.

Webb hesitated. "At that time I had found two babies in their wrong cribs," she answered, "but I couldn't exactly say earnestly that it was the same two babies."

Blakely knew that her statement clashed with the one she made earlier to the press. At that time she said she had found the Mays and Twigg babies mixed up shortly after Regina Twigg gave birth. "I looked at the babies and they were in the opposite cribs," she originally told the *St. Petersburg Times*. "I immediately changed the babies back to their own beds." Blakely knew that quote by heart, but he also knew that what Patsy Webb had admitted today was even more important. It was something Spieth denied. Webb had acknowledged not only that babies' bands frequently fell off, but also that they were simply "squeezed" back on.

"One of the most significant things the nurse's aide told me today," Blakely announced to the press as he wrapped up the depositions, "was that the bracelets not only came off, but they could be put back on."

The more John Blakely studied the medical records, the more convinced he became that the babies had been switched on purpose. For one thing, according to the charts, between December 4 and December 5, the day of the swap, the Mays baby lost six and a half ounces, making her exactly the weight that the Twigg baby had been on December 4. No weight was listed for the Twigg baby; the space was just left blank. Blakely figured it was because if the two babies' weights were simply reversed, it would make the staff suspicious and alert them to the fact that a switch had taken place.

"These charts are incredible," he told reporters, shaking his head. "They are extremely unusual. They're just one more piece of evidence that a swap occurred. Medical experts I've consulted have told me that it would be extremely unusual for a child like Kimberly to lose six and a half ounces overnight, especially because Kimberly had been steadily gaining weight since her birth six days earlier. It's also striking," he added, "that the child listed as Kimberly Mays ended up with precisely the same weight as Arlena. I'll be surprised if the doctors don't admit that these are very, very unusual weight charts."

During his deposition, Adley Sedaros agreed. He said that he did not remember the births, but he did find the weight charts unusual.

"I would look deeper into why she lost six and a half ounces in one day," he said. "Definitely, sure."

"Why was your name crossed out as the attending physician on the Mays baby's hospital charts and Dr. Palmer's name inserted?" Blakely asked.

"Probably because it was wrong to start with. This is not

my baby, it's not my patient. It's probably his patient,"
Sedaros answered.

"So you had nothing to do with any of the entries that are
contained on this page, so far as you can recall?"

"No, nothing," he repeated. "This is signed by Dr. Palmer.
This is Palmer's writing."

Blakely pointed to another note written about Barbara Coker Mays's baby dated November 29 and asked Sedaros if
that was his handwriting. When Sedaros said yes, Blakely
asked him to read it out loud.

"11/29, full-term female neonate," Sedaros began. "Delivered by C-section after manifestation of fetal distress by the
monitor. Apgar score was eight to nine, suction of the stomach contents was done, color improved . . ." Sedaros stammered, "The copy is very . . ."

"Yes," Blakely interrupted. "Please take your time."

"Color improved rapidly to become pink except for peripheral cyanosis."

"When we talk about peripheral cyanosis what are we talking about?" Blakely asked. "Would you describe that condition?"

"Partial blueness, blue color of the extremities, the face, the
feet, the hands."

Blakely nodded, satisfied. He had succeeded in pointing
out that the Mays baby was blue at birth and, more important, that the doctors obviously knew.

"Thank you," he said. "Let me ask you to turn your attention to page thirteen of the records before you. There is a
notation at nine P.M. on 11/29/78 [about the Mays baby] that
reads, 'Very active, crying at intervals, Dr. Sedaros called,
asked about baby.' Do you see that note?"

"Yes."

"If this child was not under your care as you've stated
earlier, why would the nurses call you to ask you about this
child?"

"I don't know."

"All right," Blakely said. "Then let me ask you to turn your attention to the newborn Twigg chart in the middle of the page, opposite the date 12/5. Is that note in your handwriting?"

"Yes."

"Would you read that note for us?"

"Grade three over six systolic heart murmur over left order of the sternum, possible VSD."

"All right, sir. Now what is the significance of the three over six systolic murmur?" Blakely asked.

"Moderate intensity," Sedaros answered, looking uncomfortable.

"Did this present you with some concern about the cardiac integrity of this child?" Blakely said.

"Yes," Sedaros responded solemnly.

"And what does the term 'possible VSD' mean?" Blakely asked.

"Possible means possible," Sedaros snapped, obviously agitated. "VSD is ventricular septal defect."

"And would you describe to us what a ventricular septal defect is?" Blakely said.

"It's a defect or a hole in the septum between the two ventricles. Sometimes there's a hole there."

"All right. Now this particular baby, this was the Twigg baby." Blakely paused to study the notes. "This was also Dr. Palmer's baby, was it not?"

Sedaros nodded.

"Then tell me, Doctor, how did you come to attend her and perform an examination on her on December 5, 1978?"

"I must be asked to see that baby," Sedaros answered. "I must be asked by Dr. Palmer or somebody else to see that baby."

"All right," Blakely said, appearing to accept the answer. "Turning our attention to the next page opposite the date

12/5 and the hour eight-thirty A.M., there's a note which be-gins, 'EKG.' Is that note also in your handwriting?''

"Yes."

"Would you read that note for us please?"

Sedaros sighed. "EKG, stat, chest x-rays *today*, heel stick, blood gases."

"And why were you concerned to have an EKG done on this child as soon as possible?"

"Because of the heart murmur," he answered impatiently.

"And would you tell us, Dr. Sedaros, why you wanted to have blood gases done on this particular child?"

"To check the oxygenation of the blood, the degree of oxygenation."

"Okay," Blakely said. "Down below that entry there's another entry by Dr. Palmer for 12/5 that says, 'Omit blood gases,' and then it says, 'To my office for x-rays.' Would it have been unusual for Dr. Palmer to have reversed your instructions?"

Sedaros shifted in his chair, then cleared his throat. "A little unusual," he admitted.

"Dr. Sedaros," Blakely asked, changing the line of questioning again. "Do you know Merle Coker?"

"No," he answered abruptly.

"Did you read a newspaper article that appeared in the *Miami Herald* several months ago regarding you and your personal finances or the mortgage on your house, or lien on your house in Wauchula while you lived there?"

"No," Sedaros answered again.

"I have no other questions today," Blakely said, content for the moment just to hint at the possible connections and motivations, just to make Sedaros aware that he knew they might exist.

When compensation fund attorney Kelly Joe Schmedt questioned Sedaros the next day, he seemed more collected.

His name was on the baby's chart, he explained, because he was the only pediatrician at the hospital and the clerks routinely put his name down whenever a pediatrician was called for. Sedaros also said that since C-section babies were high risk he might have called just to make sure that the baby was fine. Most of all Sedaros wanted the hospital attorneys to know that he was not actually diagnosing the Twigg baby's heart murmur on December 5. Instead, he said, he was "probably" called in as an expert to confirm Palmer's diagnosis.

They were small distinctions, but they were important ones, because what Sedaros was really saying was that the actual switch must have taken place sometime before he had examined the Twiggs' baby for the first time.

Chapter 30

The Theory

John Blakely was still hoping for someone who remembered caring for the babies and was willing to admit it. But the most he seemed to be able to establish was a connection with the Cokers.

"At any time have you personally known any member of Barbara Mays's family?" he asked Ernest Palmer.

"Yes sir," Palmer answered.

"Who?" Blakely asked.

"Larry Coker, I believe, is her brother," Palmer said.

"Any other members of her family?"

"Yes," Palmer acknowledged. "They tell me that I treated the Mays child's mother, but I don't know her name and I think she has not seen me in a long time."

"All right. Is Larry Coker a good friend of yours?"

"No sir," Palmer said.

"Is he a patient?"

"He's a patient."

"Is that the only contact through which you know him?" Blakely asked.

"Yes sir."

Blakely paused for a moment and glanced down at a sheet of paper that had been given to him by a private investigator. He read silently, "Larry and Carolyn Coker have children the same ages as Dr. Palmer's. The Palmer children and the Coker children are in fact friends; they visit each other on a more-than-regular basis. . . . Sonny Coker, who is presumed to be another relative of Barbara Mays, is the supervisor of elections in Hardee County. Larry Coker is married to Carolyn Coker and Carolyn is the county tax assessor in Hardee County."

Blakely continued his questioning. "Dr. Palmer, is that your signature in the lower right-hand corner on page one of the chart for the newborn Mays baby?"

"Yes sir."

"Are those your checkmarks, indicating that a disease had been found and you had informed the patient?"

"Yes sir."

"All right, can you tell me why you checked that, I mean made those marks there? Does that mean the Mays child had some disease upon delivery?"

"That's right."

"What diseases did the child have?"

"Had a heart murmur," Palmer answered.

"The newborn *Mays* child did," Blakely repeated, emphasizing the word Mays.

"No, I guess not." Palmer answered. "Maybe it was the other one. This is perhaps due to the C-section, I don't know, or maybe it's just a mistake."

"When did you last review this record, Dr. Palmer?" Blakely asked patiently.

"Last night," Palmer answered.

"Is it true, based on your review of this chart, that you gave a verbal order to omit the blood gases that had been ordered by Dr. Sedaros?"

"Yes," Palmer said.

"Could you tell me why?"

"No," Palmer responded, "I don't know why I did it."

"Could you tell me why a weight was not taken on the date of discharge?"

"I'd modified that to say no weight was recorded. I don't know if there was a weight taken or not."

"Should there have been?" Blakely asked.

"Yes sir, I think there should be," he replied.

Then Blakely held up a page from the hospital records and pointed to a line that had obviously been altered. "Dr. Palmer," he said, "do you have any idea what's behind the White Out in the left-hand column of this hospital chart?"

"Probably the wrong date."

Then Blakely held up Palmer's office records and pointed out that they too had been altered. "Now, Dr. Palmer," he repeated, "can you tell me what was whited out over here?"

"I think it was a six and a half changed to a six and a fourth, perhaps. I really don't know," Palmer managed.

Blakely looked down at the chart and up at Palmer again, shaking his head. "It appears to me," he said, "that whatever was typed in there that was whited out was typed in more than just one time, you see what I'm saying. Would it have been unusual to have typed 'one half' in there ten times?"

"Seems unusual to me, like, right now," Palmer stammered. "Very unusual."

Blakely shook his head again. He paused and then he sat down. The facts in this case were amazing. If he had been prosecuting a case based on allegations of an intentional swap, he might have summarized his closing argument to the jury by saying, "Ladies and Gentlemen of the Jury. Let's look at the facts. The hospital records show that the baby Barbara Coker Mays gave birth to had blue extremities, poor circulation and type B blood, just like Arlena. The hospital records show that the caesarean section was performed because this baby was already experiencing cardiac distress. The hospital records also show that Dr. Black was called in to look at the fetal monitor and was concerned enough about the baby's cardiac integrity to order the caesarean section.

"According to the nurse's notes recorded at seven-thirty P.M. on the evening of November 29, 1978, the evening that Barbara Mays gave birth, instead of rejoicing because her decade-long dream had finally come true, Barbara Coker Mays was 'very upset and crying, with Bob Mays at her side.'

"Ladies and Gentlemen, Barbara Coker Mays saw her own sick baby for feedings *every* four hours for four days before the baby was exchanged with Regina Twigg's healthy baby. In an old baby book that Cindy Tanner Mays found out in the shed, Barbara had listed the color of her baby's hair as brown, but the baby she took home from the hospital had strawberry blond hair. I ask you, Ladies and Gentlemen, is it possible that she didn't notice? Or is it possible that after ten long years of trying to have a baby, she wanted a healthy one so badly that she didn't care?

"Dr. Palmer, who had been called in to oversee the delivery, was a family physician to the Coker clan. Ladies and Gentlemen, I ask you, was it simply a coincidence that he canceled the blood gas test on December 5, 1978, the test that would have revealed that the babies had already been switched? Was it also a coincidence that the doctor who confirmed the diagnosis of heart disease after the babies had been switched was being sued by seven construction companies and needed money?"

"Ladies and Gentlemen of the Jury, use your heads. The hospital records have been whited out and changed. Critical information about the babies' weights has been omitted. Dr. Palmer's office records have also been whited out and changed. Even Arlena's birth certificate has been altered. Under birth defects the word 'none' has been flagrantly crossed out and the words 'congenital heart disease' have been written in by hand."

"Today we have a new piece of evidence. Today Patsy Webb, an aide, has finally admitted that despite their permanent clasps, the babies' identification bracelets could actually be slipped on and off quite easily. Is it a coincidence that the physical description of the woman who allegedly entered a Circle K store and told Kathryn Drevermann, 'I was ordered to switch those bands from one baby to the other' matches that of Patsy Webb? Ladies and Gentlemen, is it simply a coincidence that another aide claims she was sent home from the maternity ward and later warned not to talk?

"Are all these facts coincidences? You think about it. A young woman from a prominent family had been trying for ten years to have a baby. She finally gave birth to a child who was not expected to live for more than a week or two. The doctors and nurses wanted to help, but no one knew how.

"Three days later a poor woman with six previous children came into the hospital and delivered another little girl. This child was healthy, but by chance hospital records showed that her last baby daughter had died from a heart condition at the age of six weeks. Suddenly there was a way to give Bob and Barbara Mays a healthy baby girl to take home. All somebody had to do was switch the little girls' identification bands and change the medical records and birth certificates.

"The poor mother with five other children could simply be told that this baby had a heart condition just like her last one. But who would change the bands? We know that somehow they did get changed. Was that a coincidence too? Or was there a deliberate and methodical plan to switch these two babies?"

John Blakely knew all of these coincidences pointed to an intentional swap, but he couldn't pursue them without jeopardizing the civil suit against the hospital.

"Thank you, Dr. Palmer," he said, satisfied for the moment. He believed that these charts and records would serve him well when he went back to Judge Owens. Whether or not Palmer himself was responsible for the changes was not a question he needed to explore. He simply wanted to establish the existence of enough discrepancies to convince Judge Owens that a blood test was warranted, and he felt he had done that.

The courts didn't see it that way. The more it looked like Kimberly Mays belonged to the Twiggs the less they wanted to cooperate.

On March 22, 1989, the Second District Court of Appeals sided with Bob Mays. Their opinion stated that genetic testing of Kimberly would cause unjustified humiliation and psychological damage. Admittedly natural parents have certain presumed rights of custody to their own offspring; however, those rights are not absolute. Children are not property but individuals whose needs and physical and mental well-being find protection in the law.

"The Appeals Court agrees with me," Ginsberg announced. "If the court finds that allowing the Twiggs to move further is detrimental to the child, then the case is over. There's no additional discovery and no blood test."

The *St. Petersburg Times* applauded the decision, saying that Bob, who had "raised Kimberly alone since her mother's death in 1981, finally had reason to hope that the ruling signaled a turning point in the uncertainty swirling around the family."

The *Orlando Sentinel* agreed. "The courts have ruled wisely in the Kimberly Mays case and it's a time for common sense to prevail. Ernest and Regina Twigg have subjected the little girl and the only father she has ever known to untold agonies and uncertainty. . . . If they back away now and explain that their fierce love overcame their good judgment, she might one day understand why they put her through such torment."

"I'm thrilled," Bob said. "Everybody's been asking me what I want for my birthday. I kept saying a break in the case. Well now I've got it."

That night at a small, private celebration, he announced his plans to marry Darlena Sousa and said that Kimberly was delighted to be getting a new mother.

Blakely took the court ruling hard. "It's not going to stop the proceedings. It's just going to make them more costly, more time consuming and more intrusive for everyone. I'm going to ask the entire appellate court of twelve judges to reconsider the opinion, and if that fails, I'll take the case to the Florida Supreme Court. This ruling seems to totally ignore the rights and feelings and anguish of Mr. and Mrs. Twigg. They shouldn't be forced to undergo a hypothetical custody trial before learning the identity of the child. They have a right to learn what happened to their daughter and to decide who should have custody of her."

The Voice of
Regina Twigg

We decided to go back to the lower court and try to prove to Judge Owens that we wouldn't harm Kimberly. First John Blakely was going to depose Robert Mays. Then he was going to call Bob Mays's second wife, Cindy. Shortly after Mays heard that Cindy was being deposed he did a complete turnaround.

"Hey," he said. "Let's all get together and talk about this."

For the first time I would stand face to face with the man who had custody of my child, the man who had been fighting against me for more than a year. I hated to go and meet him without Ernest at my side, but Ernest couldn't get any more time off from work. He'd already missed too much. When John picked me up that morning, I'd been crying and crying. I knew that I was too upset to express myself as I would want to, so I decided to just let John do all the talking.

We all sat around a table in a meeting room in the Sarasota Courthouse. Bob Mays started off. "Kimberly's of an age when she likes to visit her friends on the weekends," he said, "so I don't think there's really any time for visitation."

"Well, she'll be twelve and fourteen and sixteen and old enough to make her own decisions soon," Ginsberg added.

John saw the pattern. "Hey, the Cokers weren't allowed to see the child for four and a half years after Bob and Cindy were married. Then when they were divorced, Cindy, who raised Kimberly, was prevented from having any relationship or contact."

Mays grinned. "Well," he said, "meeting Mrs. Twigg here for the first time like this, I can honestly say I would not be opposed to having Kimberly spend time with *her.*"

He seemed to be either approving of me or trying to con me. I didn't know which, but I didn't dare utter a word because I was afraid I would lose control and express my anger.

During a break, when John and I went out of the meeting, he said, "Regina, let's consider an agreement that will allow you to get the genetic testing on Kimberly now. If we don't make some agreement with Mays, Kimberly might be an adult before you learn whether she's really your child. Mays says he'll agree to allow the testing if you'll promise not to ask for custody now. That compromise should be acceptable to you because it might not be enforceable. Besides, if the testing proves she's yours and visitation leads Kimberly to ask for more contact, you might end up with custody anyway."

I told him I didn't want to drop the custody issue. "John," I said, "I don't want my daughter to feel for one minute that I've given up on her."

"But Regina, if we get into a prolonged custody battle, Kimberly is the one who will really be hurt, and you'll be perceived as the villain." He convinced me that his proposal would be easier on Kimberly and that it was the only chance we had to get Bob Mays to agree to the genetic testing.

Back in the meeting room, John said, "Well, let's see if we can get this worked out. Ernest and Regina don't want to uproot Kimberly if she is in a happy home. We'll relinquish the custody fight if you'll agree to the blood test." Mays raised his eyebrows and smiled. Then he said he wanted it in writing. John worked on it all week. The agreement he put together stated that during the ongoing lawsuit we would not pursue custody even if she were our child unless Bob Mays was found to be an unfit parent or there was an extreme change of circumstances. Mays approved it.

We were supposed to sign the document and then get the genetic testing done. I wanted very much to reassure Kimberly that we would never snatch her away or frighten her. At the same time, signing that agreement was a very hard thing for me to do. My mother had signed me away under duress and now I felt like I was doing the same thing. When we met at John's office to sign it, I just sat there and sat there.

Finally I reached out for the document. It was one of the hardest things I can ever remember doing.

Chapter 31

The Blood Test

"Praise the Good Lord, this will be the best thing for that child," Velma Coker said, wiping her eyes when she heard about the agreement. "This whole thing has affected Kimberly a lot more than anyone realizes. When she looks up at me with those eyes and says, 'Granny, what's going to happen to me?' it tears my heart out."

"If Kimberly turns out to be the Twiggs' biological child," St. Petersburg psychologist William Hafling said, "she will learn something that a lot of people don't know. She will learn that there's a biological parent and there's a *real* parent and they're not necessarily the same people."

"Except for some anxiety about getting her blood drawn with a needle, Kimberly's delighted," Bob stated. "There's not some awesome shadow in the background trying to grab her anymore."

The Cokers had also agreed to be tested to determine Barbara's genetic makeup. Velma, a thin woman with short graying hair, glasses and a withered face, smiled tensely when Kimberly, Bob and Darlena arrived at the lab in Sarasota.

Kimberly was as sparkly and sweet and pretty as ever in her short skirt and sneakers, with her hair in a ponytail. But when she saw the needle she began to get frightened. "Is that needle and tube going to be filled with my blood?" she asked, leaning against Velma for support. When she watched Bob's blood filling a tube she really got scared. The Cokers were next. By the time it was her turn she was hysterical. "I'm afraid, I'm afraid!" she cried. "I don't want to do it!" She ran to Velma, then to Darlena, then to Bob. "Daddy, Daddy, why do I have to do it?" she wept. But it was strictly the needle she was upset about. Finally, they all held her. Afterward she laughed a beautiful, bubbly little-girl laugh and talked about how silly it was to have been so afraid. Then she hugged everyone, smiled and posed for a photograph.

Chapter 32

The Result

"Hey, Regina," John Blakely said with a gleeful lilt in his voice when he called from California three weeks later. "How are you doing?"

"I'm climbing the walls. I can hardly wait till the tests come back."

"Well, they came back early," he drawled in that easygoing, smooth way of his. Regina drew in her breath.

"Want to know what they said?"

Regina still couldn't speak.

"She's a Twigg all the way."

"Oh, thank God!" Regina screamed, jumping up and down. "Ernest, she's ours. She's ours."

"She's our sister," Normia yelled. Suddenly, all the kids were also jumping up and down and laughing and crying. "It's her, it's her, we found her, we found our sister."

Ernest picked Regina up and kissed her. "I knew it," he said. "She's ours, babe, she's ours."

By Sunday, at the press conference, Regina was calm again. She just sat there and smiled quietly until Blakely announced the results of the test to the world. Then her eyes filled with tears. "At last there's some sunshine. Nothing can bring back our Arlena or the years we lost with our Kimberly," Regina told the crowd of reporters. "But I'm glad the blood test is done and that we finally know for sure."

"These are the sisters and brothers of Kimberly Michelle Mays," Blakely added cheerfully as the seven Twigg children marched through the tangle of cameras and lights.

Within hours a hundred different shows from as far away as England, Australia, Germany and Japan were requesting TV and radio appearances. Blakely had to hire extra help just to handle the calls. There was no way the Twiggs could appear on all those shows, so he chose *The Oprah Winfrey Show*, then agreed to an appearance on *Larry King Live* because it was on CNN and he figured it probably had an international audience. Regina liked Oprah best. There was something about the way Oprah squeezed her hand when they talked about Arlena that made Regina feel she really cared.

Just a few hours after appearing before twenty million people, Ernest was back at the dilapidated pink stucco Amtrak station in Sebring. As usual he was there when the trains pulled in, to sell tickets, to check baggage and to make reservations. As Ernest sat alone in his booth, he watched a stranger near the empty tracks reading the headlines about his family. "Lots of folks around here don't know me," he explained to some reporters from the *Tampa Tribune* who stopped by that evening to interview him. "We've just come back to town here, you know, after several years of living in Pennsylvania. Our friends have been real supportive and some of the people who work at Amtrak have called to say, 'We're with you.' But others wonder why we're pursuing this. I guess you'd have to be a parent to know why."

On Wednesday, after returning from a long-weekend boating trip, Bob made his first public appearance since getting the test results. "First we sat together on her bed after she returned home from school Friday," he told the throng of reporters jamming his attorney's office. "She knew something was wrong by the look on my face.

" 'Am I your daughter?' she asked.

" 'You'll always be my daughter,' I told her, 'but the tests show you're not my biological daughter.'

"She cried and hugged me, sobbing, 'Oh, Daddy, oh, Daddy. What does this mean? What does this mean?'

"She still calls me Daddy, and I certainly am her dad. We're just going to take it more or less one step at a time and continue to reinforce the idea that nothing is going to change as far as she and I are concerned. But now that she knows she has another family, she'll have to decide whether she's interested in meeting them. I don't intend to influence her decision; I just want to concentrate on making her as happy as possible. For the first time in her young life this is *her* decision. I'm not saying it's an easy one. I was perfectly happy with our life prior to this, and I think she was too. I've assured Kimberly that I will support her even if she chooses to spend a lot of time with the Twiggs. That might be difficult for me, but I will try to put her feelings ahead of mine. We've got to make every effort to make this child as comfortable as possible with what she wants."

Now more than ever the press applauded Bob. "She was raised by a loving father," the *Sarasota Herald Tribune* wrote, "who from all appearances has assiduously provided a secure, stable home. She reportedly is well adjusted socially and at school. . . . For those assets she can be grateful to Robert Mays, the man she calls Daddy; so can her biological parents, Mr. and Mrs. Twigg, appreciate the exemplary parenting she has received."

"If you believe in divine providence," the *Gondolier* echoed, "you can rationalize that it was meant the Twiggs with seven other children should spare one for a man who otherwise would have had neither wife nor child." They didn't know that Bob was about to marry his third wife, Darlena.

It was a small Saturday afternoon wedding in February 1990 at the Prince of Peace Lutheran Church. A few days before the ceremony, Bob told the press that he had been involved with Darlena Sousa for several years. "She has helped me and Kimberly to weather the emotional storm surrounding the swap. Kimberly is thrilled," he said. "First we'll accept each other and then we'll accept her. We're all going to exchange rings. Kimberly's going to play a big part of it. This would have been a lot tougher if Darlena hadn't been around through the whole thing," he said, smiling at the surprised reporters.

The Voice of
Regina Twigg

We signed the agreement in October. Kimberly was tested in November; Thanksgiving passed. Christmas passed. The New Year began. Bob Mays remarried. Spring came and went. We were still waiting to meet Kimberly. First they were busy for the holidays; then it was the wedding. After that it was school. Then one of the reporters came to me and said, "You're a happy family. You have seven other children; he just has one. Why don't you just leave her alone?"

Bob told the press that Kim had written a note that said, "I hate the Twiggs. I wish they would go away." He called the newspapers and gave them the quote. It was printed all over the United States.

I responded by giving the press two poems that I had written. The first one was in memory of Arlena; the other expressed my love for Kimberly. I'm not a writer, but I'm proud of these poems. Proud that I found a way to express my love and my grief. I was also trying to reach Kimberly, hoping that somehow she would see the poem to her and understand that I wasn't trying to hurt her or frighten her.

Later we learned that a kid at school had cut the poem about Kimberly out of the newspaper and given it to her. She kept it with her and showed it to her friends. "It's kind of nice, don't you think?" she said.

Bob called the newspaper and blasted both poems as an insensitive publicity stunt. "All those little poems and flowery things that she makes up won't change a thing," he yelled. "I'm truly sitting here waiting for the first sign of love, true love, and I haven't seen it yet. My answer would be, 'Back off and let this child figure out what's happened here.'"

A few days later, the reporter who interviewed Bob called me and said, "Bob Mays went crazy when he saw those poems. I didn't print half the rage he flew into. It was a side of him I had never seen before. I was stunned, but since then I have talked to some other people who say they heard he has an uncontrollable temper."

"I'm sorry he had that reaction," I said. "The poems are my expression of love for both the girls, not hatred or anger for anyone."

To My Daughter Arlena

Arlena girl, I loved you then,
So short a time I held you when,
My heart breaks in utter grief,
The pain won't ease, there's no relief.

How can I e'er go on from here
Without your precious self so near?
How can I e'er expect to cope?
What is faith and where is hope?

To those who say, "Just let her go,"
'Tis not them, how judge they so?
To mourn forever is not unreal,
Other mothers know how I feel.

"Ray of Sunshine," you helped us live,
You'd always smile and say "Forgive."
They say "Go on now with your life,

Others need you, mom and wife."
To days gone by, you cannot go,
Just the LOVE, it does hurt so just to know,
Not e'er again I will not see,
Your precious self in front of me.

Not now upon this earth to be,
Perhaps my child, eternally!

To My Daughter Kimberly

Baby Girl, I loved you then,
So short a time I held you when,
Tragedy, sad tears to fall,
Life, has hurt us one and all.

Precious baby, in our arms,
We never shared your baby charms,
'Deed we know just how you feel,
'Deed we know your pain is real.

If you could but just believe,
Little one, for you we grieve,
Your seven brothers and sisters, too,
Kimberly, they hurt as you.

The world's been judging one and all,
Who knows if they'll a victim fall,
What happened that December day
Could not be simply swept away.

Truth is not best left unknown,
How would you feel when you are grown?
Lost, lonely years and sad despair,
Shattered lives, all so unfair.

"Oh," they'd say, "just go away,
This has to stop, no test today,"
Mom and Dad couldn't turn their back,
And walk away, just like that.

Love runs too deep within our lives
To mock the truth and live life's lies,
Denied the right to love us then,
We hope you'll love us someday. When?

Chapter 33

The Meeting

Bob was wearing sandals, an orange-and-pink striped shirt and blue spandex shorts. His new wife, Darlena, was at his side, dressed in khaki shorts. Everything about their demeanor said that for them this meeting was nothing, just a brief, annoying errand on the way to the boat.

After eight long months Mays had finally agreed to let Kimberly meet her sisters and brothers but not Regina and Ernest. Ernest cleared his throat. How the mental health professionals came up with this scheme was beyond him. The Twiggs and the Mayses and their court-mandated psychologists were supposed to get together in Ginsberg's office in Sarasota while all the kids met at the White Bird Miniature Golf Course, chaperoned by the secretary of the Mayses' psychiatrist, Dr. Lawrence Ritt.

Ernest thought it was called Blue Bird. Luckily, the kids started yelling from the backseat, "Daddy, that's it, that's it. You passed it." It was all Regina and Ernest could do not to wait around and get a glimpse of Kimberly, but they followed the plan and left the kids there alone, nervously waiting to meet their sister.

"I think we should all introduce ourselves and, you know, tell a little bit about our lives," Dr. Ritt said, gesturing toward the chairs and trying to be cordial.

"There's already been so much in the press I don't think I can learn any more," Bob answered sarcastically. Regina could see the anger in his eyes. "Let's just talk about what's best for Kimberly," he added. "If after a couple of visits she decides she doesn't want to continue, then she shouldn't be pushed."

"I disagree," Regina said, instantly irked.

"But I'm her parent and I have the right to make the decisions for her. Kimberly Michelle Mays is my legal daughter."

Regina calmed herself. "If Arlena had lived, it wouldn't be right for us to deprive you," she said, trying to reason with him.

"But you did deprive me," Bob snapped. "You knew she wasn't yours after that blood test and you didn't come looking for me."

"I didn't know she wasn't mine. I couldn't figure out why the blood types were different. I was afraid my husband would think I was running around."

"Well, weren't you? From the articles I read it looked like you were."

"Now wait a minute," Ernest said, standing up. "I think you'd better just calm down. That's my wife you're talking to."

"Accusing me of running around is very, very nasty and very ugly," Regina snapped angrily.

"Well, you're the one who made the statement to the media," Mays snickered, as he left for the bathroom. The door was behind the couch. In the awkward silence that followed they could hear the toilet flushing.

"Darlena," Dr. Hal Smith, the psychiatrist for the Twiggs, said, "are you against Kimberly meeting her parents?"

Regina looked at her. A girl from out West, eyes wide apart, big hips, big thighs. "Yes I am," Darlena answered. "She's very apprehensive. She's afraid that they will steal her away."

"Well, if he hadn't convinced her that we were monsters," Regina quipped, gesturing toward the bathroom, "she wouldn't be so apprehensive."

When Bob walked back in Dr. Smith said, "What's it gonna be Bob? It's been almost two years since this started and they still haven't met her."

"It could be ten for all I care!" Bob yelled.

"We want to talk to Kimberly before laying out a schedule," Dr. Ritt interjected, trying to calm things down. "It's all up to her."

"When we signed that agreement," Regina said, "it was with the understanding that we'd share parenting."

"*If* it was in Kimberly's best interest," Bob shouted. "Look," he said, "we live a *very* busy life. Over the summer Kimberly is going to be spending two weeks with each of her grandparents, she's going to summer school and we'll be out on the boat for a month with another couple."

"Well then, why don't we all just drive over right now and meet Kimberly and the other children at the golf club?" Dr. Smith suggested.

"Absolutely not, do you hear me!" Bob spat. "Do you hear me?"

"I hear you loud and clear," Dr. Smith said. "I thought we were going to let Kimberly decide."

"I am the legal father of Kimberly Michelle Mays, and I have the right to tell her what to do from one second to the next, from one minute to the next, from one hour to the next, from one month to the next, from one year to the next, till she turns eighteen, and then she can do what she wants to do!"

"Hey," Dr. Smith said, "maybe we should wrap this up and get together some other time."

"I don't think that would help," Mays retorted. "And if the adults can't get along, then it will never work out for Kimberly."

Regina had read about Bob's earlier behavior in an article in the *St. Petersburg Times*. She figured this was the same technique he had used to separate Kimberly from Cindy Mays and Ashlee and from the Cokers before that.

"Of course it won't work," she answered, her voice rising, "as long as you're so obsessively possessive of her life and her every breath." Now that Regina was all worked up, Bob seemed to calm down.

"Tell me about Arlena," he said, changing the subject.

"Well," Ernest said kind of sadly, "she was a real little homebody. She liked to cook. She was a little peacemaker too. Now if she was only here today." An image of Arlena's sweet smile flooded Regina's consciousness. She could feel herself getting close to tears.

Dr. Smith looked at her. She drew in her breath. "May I be excused?" she said like a little kid as she hurried to the bathroom with tears streaming down her cheeks. By the time she'd finished splashing water on her face, she was composed.

Meanwhile, Dr. Ritt had taken Bob aside and talked to him privately. "You know what I'm going to do," Bob said when Regina came back, "just to show you what a nice guy I really am?"

"What?" Regina said, glaring at him.

"As Kimberly's father I'm going to permit you to go over to that golf course and meet my daughter."

Chapter 34

The Children's Hour

All seven children were lined up on a bench waiting nervously. When the car pulled up at the putt-putt golf range, Kimberly was peering out of the window breathing deeply. As soon as she got out of the car Irisa went up to her. She smiled and said, "Are you Kim?"

"Yes," Kimberly answered.

"I'm Irisa," she said, and hugged her.

"I'm Normia," Normia managed. Then all of a sudden she was bawling.

"Oh, don't cry," Kimberly said, reaching out and hugging her. That really broke the ice.

"I guess we're all nervous," Kimberly added sweetly. Her eyes sparkled. She seemed happy, even ecstatic. She looked just like Normia did in the picture taken when she was eleven years old. The Twigg children went around and told Kimberly who they were. They thought they'd have trouble getting Barry to talk, but they didn't. Kimberly just had a way about her that made them all comfortable. "I'm Barry and I'm in kindergarten," he said. Even Tommy, Ernie and

Will liked her. She looked so pretty in her knee-length shorts and her green-and-black shirt. But mostly it was her smile, and something else that they all felt inside but couldn't pin down.

They all giggled together and made small talk. Kimberly told them she liked spaghetti and oldies music. And when Irisa told her she was going to have a baby, she jumped up and down saying, "I'm going to be an aunt, I'm going to be an aunt."

"Be careful," Kimberly kept saying after that. "I want to have a perfect little niece. Maybe it will be born on my birthday, November twenty-ninth."

"No, honey," Irisa said, "that's not your birthday. That's Arlena's birthday."

"Oh gosh, that's right," Kimberly said, then her face clouded over. "I'm all confused."

After that they played putt-putt golf. "I wish I could stay all day," Kim said, "but my dad has plans. I have to go out on the boat." Then she asked the secretary to call Dr. Ritt's office to see if she could stay a little longer. "But please don't say that I wanted it to be longer," she whispered. "Please say it was the kids who want me to stay longer."

"Dr. Ritt wants to talk to you," the secretary said a minute later, handing the phone to Kim.

"How would you like to meet Mr. and Mrs. Twigg?" he asked.

"Oh my goodness. Oh my gosh," Kimberly stammered. Then she looked at the children and took a deep breath. "Yes," she said, "I'd like that."

Chapter 35

Reunion

Regina was holding Ernest's hand. Her eyes were riveted on the child. She was transfixed by the little girl in the distance sitting at the picnic table. Kimberly was coming into focus now. The little ponytail, the shape of her face, her nose, her long, beautiful legs. Kimberly saw them coming, and turned and walked toward them, extending her hand. Bob, Darlena, Dr. Ritt and Dr. Smith were a little bit behind. Regina opened her arms, her eyes filled with tears. "Can I have a great big hug?" she managed. Kimberly looked right at her. Their eyes met; Kim's were clear and green, just like Regina's. "Yes," she said, "you can."

Regina felt the child in her arms and a small hand patting her back. Regina straightened up. Sniffling, with tears splashing down her cheeks, she smiled and looked at Kimberly. "Well," she said, "it's been a long time."

"Yes," the child answered. "All my life, in fact!" Then Kimberly stood there like a beautiful little debutante, sparkling, poised, bubbly, shining. Ernest hung back, afraid of overwhelming her or himself, half choked by his own emotion.

"Kimberly," Bob interrupted, breaking the spell, "I'd like you to meet Mr. and Mrs. Twigg." Kimberly looked nervously at him then back at Irisa and the kids.

There was an exquisite sensitivity about this child, and she felt an almost magnetic pull toward the stranger who was her mother.

"That's such a pretty dress," Kimberly said, in her lovely bell-like voice. All the while her eyes said "Mother, Mother, my real mother." Regina intuitively received the message. She smiled that radiant smile of hers. Her eyes danced across the faces of her children, together for the first time. "All these green eyes," she breathed.

Darlena glared at her, but Regina was past that. Those daggers were nothing.

Regina and the girls played a game of putt-putt golf. Kimberly edged toward Regina, handed her a golf ball and said, "Here, Mom."

"You have two moms now," Regina said, "me and Darlena. You can call me Mom Twigg, if you're comfortable with that."

"I'll just call you Mom," Kimberly answered, "except when he's around, then I'll call you Mrs. Twigg."

Three or four times while they were playing, Kimberly hugged her. "Here, Mom," she said, "here's the ball. When I grow up," she volunteered shyly, "I'm going to be a baby doctor and make sure there are no switches. And I'm going to have eight kids, just like you." They were all drawn to each other—mother, father, daughter, sisters and brothers. She had a kind of beauty, Regina thought. It was not a striking beauty, and yet it was. Regina was absolutely, utterly fascinated, as if the eleven years of absence had created a kind of unnamed hunger that needed to be satisfied.

Bob and Darlena approached and said it was time to get a picture taken. Kimberly was much more withdrawn in their presence. He was holding her hand now, squeezing it tightly. "Are you ready to come down now from cloud nine?" Regina heard him say.

After the picture was taken, Regina knelt down. She put her hands on Kimberly's shoulders. "I love you Kimberly, and I always will." Their eyes held in a long, penetrating gaze. Kimberly didn't say anything. Suddenly there was fear in her eyes. When Regina looked up she saw Bob Mays standing right above them.

Chapter 36

Goodbye Again

They saw Kimberly three more times. Each time they planned an activity. They went to the beach, they went bowling and they went roller skating. Sarasota was a two-hour drive from Sebring, so they never had enough time to bring Kim home. They wanted to keep things light and give her a chance to get to know them without a lot of tension. Funny thing was that in a way she seemed to know them already. Not in the everyday details of their lives, but in some way that went deeper. At the beginning of each visit she sparkled. That was the only word for it. She actually seemed to glow. Then, as they got closer to the time of separation, she'd become depressed, almost despondent.

"Kimberly," Regina said, on their way to meet Regina's friend Betty Parker, "I hope you're being well cared for and that people love you and you love them."

"Well, you all love me," Kimberly answered evasively, toying with her hair. Later, when Betty asked her what she thought when she first saw her brothers and sisters, Kimberly answered, "I just thought to myself, they're so pretty. They're so beautiful."

"And your mom and dad?" Betty asked.

Kimberly paused, then sighed. "At last my long-lost parents, my real mom and dad," she said.

"Kimberly," Regina interrupted, wanting to be sure the child didn't feel pushed. "We always want you to love the special others in your life."

"But you're blood," Kimberly answered. "You're my blood."

Another time when they went bowling, Kimberly asked Regina if she should put her name down on the bowling list as Arlena or Kimberly.

"Why would you write Arlena?" Regina asked.

"Well, that's what you really meant to name me," Kimberly explained.

"Honey," Regina said, "we love you whatever your name is. Long ago, when I was a little girl, my name was Mary Lee. That's really still my name. You can be KimberLee if you want to. Then our names will kind of match. Kimberly, we want you to understand that we never gave you away and we're never going to turn our back on you."

"Well my dad says that after a while, I'll just be one of the bunch and you won't think I'm special anymore."

"We'll always think you are special," Regina said. As they drove toward the parking lot to meet Bob Mays, Regina was suddenly struck by a feeling that she couldn't explain. "Listen Kimberly," she said with urgency in her voice. "He may get mad at us and not let us see you again. It might be a long time, we might have to go back to court and it might be a tough battle. Take our phone number. Keep it in a safe place."

"I'll hide it," she said softly. They could see Bob's car in the distance. The headlights were on, the engine running.

"Always remember that we love you very much," Regina said.

Kimberly looked straight into Regina's eyes and held her hand tightly. "I'll tell you a secret, Mom," she whispered. "I love you too. I love all of you." Then Kimberly opened the car door and disappeared into the darkness. That was the last time they ever saw her.

Part VI

EPILOGUE

Mother is the
name for God in
the lips and
hearts of little
children.

WILLIAM
MAKEPEACE
THACKERAY

Chapter 37

Kimberly

In October 1990, Bob Mays unilaterally cut off all visitation and phone contact. At first he said he was punishing Kimberly because her grades had slipped. Then he said it was because she was depressed and had been placed on medication. Later he claimed it was because she was exhibiting "attitude problems" and it took him two or three days to calm her down after each visit.

For the Twiggs, these have been difficult years filled with court hearings, countless depositions, unsuccessful mediation and canceled court dates. Recently the Twiggs told John Blakely to begin preparing for a custody battle. Cindy Mays and Dr. Stephen Groff were subpoenaed. Neither of them was willing to come forward unless ordered to by the judge.

Blakely started off very slowly. "Cindy," he said, "this is going to be hard. Just look at me. Keep your eyes on me alone as if there's nobody else here."

For a second, inadvertently, she turned. The court reporter was to the right, then Arthur Ginsberg, then Bob Mays staring at her. Attorneys from the hospital were next to him. All of them were sitting around one table in John Blakely's Tampa office as if they were about to order dinner. Cindy shivered, then turned to the left again and locked her eyes on Blakely's. She had been feeling stronger each week, and except for a couple of anxiety attacks right before the deposition started, she was in good control.

She was thinner and looked pretty in her black skirt, a white-and-black polka-dot top that flared at the waist, a red pocket scarf, white silk pantyhose, black heels and red earrings. She knew Bob would notice, and she wasn't about to give him the satisfaction of seeing her looking anything but her best.

Blakely had gone over everything with her for an hour and a half the night before, then again briefly in the morning. He had heard about Bob's drinking, his ridiculing Kim and kicking her. He had heard about Bob throwing Kim across the room. He had heard about Bob pulling out a gun and threatening to shoot Cindy. He'd thought he had heard everything, but the puppies still surprised him. The thought of a grown man threatening to shoot his own kid's puppies was deeply disturbing.

"Did Mr. Mays ever threaten to kill anyone besides you in the bedroom?" he asked.

"After we moved into our house in Riverview," Cindy said, "Bob brought home two puppies one time, then he brought another puppy home. They started digging out underneath the fence. I heard the kids screaming. I ran out. Bob was getting the gun to kill them."

"Was he expressing out loud that he intended to kill them?" Blakely asked, surprised.

"Yes sir," Cindy answered.

"And were the children crying?"

"Yes sir," she said.

For four hours, Cindy Tanner Mays held her own. She didn't even look at Bob again until she got to the part about

Kimberly leaving for the last time. Then she glanced over. She saw him right there at the table, furiously scribbling on a yellow legal pad, so close she could almost touch him. Cindy took a deep breath.

"He sat the two girls down on the couch and said that we couldn't make it," she whispered. "That he was moving; he was taking Kimberly. So a friend of his came up and helped him, and he took her. He put her in the car. She was crying. She wanted her mother. She didn't want to leave. I was the only mom she's ever known. I can't tell you what it's been like without her."

Cindy's voice broke. She put her face in her hands and cried. When she looked up at Blakely he actually had tears in his eyes. "Are you okay?" he said. "Do you want to take a five-minute break?"

"Yeah," she answered, wiping her eyes with the red handkerchief.

Ginsberg came walking up to Blakely during the break. His face was bright red. "I don't know why you're doing this," he snarled. "She's just being vindictive. My client denies all of this."

Seven months later, on May 2, 1991, John Blakely and Arthur Ginsberg stood before Judge Owens again, still arguing over the right to call Dr. Stephen Groff and break the patient-physician confidentiality privilege on the grounds that it was outweighed by Kimberly's best interests.

"The only question now," Ginsberg said, "is what's in the best interest of this child as far as visiting the Twiggs. It's not whether Mr. Mays is a good father or is not a good father. That's got nothing to do with what's before the court at this time. Clearly they're after requesting some type of visitation schedule," he continued, "and we're still working on that.

"I don't think that things that happened in 1987 are relevant to something that's going on in 1991."

"Judge," John Blakely said with quiet determination in his

voice, "we have spent hundreds of thousands of dollars getting to this point and the first issue really before the court today is if this information is relevant. The second issue is, if it is relevant, do I need to file another separate petition before I take the deposition?

"The fact is," Blakely continued, "that what Dr. Groff has to say is extremely relevant, because it will prove that Kimberly had problems with school and with behavior from kindergarten on, and that it has nothing to do with seeing the Twiggs."

Owens seemed to agree at least in theory. Just the same, everyone was told to try to work things out once again before calling Dr. Groff. Eight more months passed. Bob Mays wouldn't budge. There was still no contact with Kimberly.

On January 24, 1992, fifteen months after their last visit with Kimberly, at the order of the judge Stephen Groff was finally deposed in his office in Tampa. He was the most important witness Blakely had, a well-respected neuropsychiatrist with a special expertise in the area of pediatric attention-deficit disorders, hyperactivity and school refusal. He'd seen the whole family for six months before the separation and had continued to see Bob privately afterward. If Stephen Groff confirmed what Cindy Mays had said, there would be no way for Ginsberg to discredit her.

Stephen Groff handed out typed copies of the notes he had taken during the actual sessions to both attorneys, then began to summarize them: "In short, they were having problems, and they all seemed to circle around their arguments concerning Bob's treatment of Kimberly. The essence of it was—and it doesn't say it there, but I know this—that Bob was being physical with Kimberly, and Cindy didn't like it . . .

"She's failing at school . . . and the school recommended a psychologist, but Bob refuses to let the child see a psychologist . . . I wrote down 'He believes in beating her,' and that gives a poor result. . . . That's what they disagree about.

"The last sentence [on November 5] says, 'Bob picking on everyone at home when he's in one of his moods. Calls Kimberly dumb, stupid. Whipping on legs and behind.' "

"Does he deny that?" Blakely asked.

"No," Groff answered.

On February 6, Groff met alone with Kimberly to make a psychological evaluation. Looking at his notes again, he said, "I would professionally say that this child is normal. This child does not have attention-deficit disorder with or without hyperactivity. . . . The cause of her problems is the father's physical behavior toward the child.

"It's my specific recollection," Groff said, "as I sit here now, that if I were to characterize Bob to you as I had known him over this period of time, that Bob always had some disagreement with either the Cokers, his own parents, Cindy, the schoolteachers, the therapists. He had a difference of opinion about how Kimberly should be raised or physically treated with everybody I had ever come across in my discussions with him. This leads him to get very disturbed and angry with these people. If they differ with him, he would deny them visitation, deny them seeing her. And this is a theme that repeats itself throughout the entire time I knew Bob."

Groff looked at Blakely and said pointedly, "Now I know he's denying your clients, the Twiggs, visitation. And so it seems to me that it's very consistent with something he always does."

Groff went back to his notes. "March 20 . . . oh, this is a historical session. There's a star there," he added, glancing over at Ginsberg, who was staring intently at him.

"What happened in that session is now very clear to me. Cindy and Bob were at a point where she was saying, you know, 'You're really beating the child too much. That's got to stop.' And Cindy related to me this most recent episode of him beating the child, and he was furious. They were hardly talking to each other, they were so angry. They were fuming. She said, 'You really walloped that child and hit her hard.' And he said, 'I did not.' So Cindy said, 'Why don't you show Dr. Groff how you hit the child?' At which time he stood up and bashed his fist on this glass.' '' Groff gestured toward the glass coffee table in front of them. ''I thought he was going to break the table—flat hand, palm down, he smashed his fist on that thing. And he got up and left.''

''Did you say anything to him before he left?'' Blakely asked.

''As he was leaving I made the appropriate psychiatric interpretation of, 'Bob, you ought to stay and talk.' But when a person is in the state that he was, he's extremely intimidating and explosive, and Bob is not a tiny person. I mean, he's a good-sized person. He left, and I was left there sitting with Cindy, and that's what happened in that session.''

''Did he hit the table harder than in your opinion he should hit a child for disciplinary purposes?'' Blakely asked.

''He hit that table so hard that I was grateful that it's a half-inch-thick glass,'' Groff answered, ''and I was amazed that he didn't break his hand . . .''

''If he hits Kimberly as hard as he hits the table, would that constitute child abuse?''

''Yes,'' Groff answered. Blakely frowned. It was a victory, but one without joy.

Groff again referred to his notes. ''On the entry of April 15, 1986, it says, 'Bob wants to totally control [Kimberly and Cindy]' . . . and his severe personality disorder 'has little chance for change with therapy.'

''So what I'm saying is that the prognosis, even with any therapy, is quite poor.''

"Is this disorder something that actually has a name to it, or is it just the way he is reacting with Kimberly?" Blakely asked, ignoring Ginsberg's glare.

"No, no, this is not a pejorative," Groff said. "This is a diagnosis out of the *Diagnostic and Statistical Manual.* The personality disorders have always been diagnosed in psychiatric manuals. In the old gray manual going back fifteen years, the personality disorder that I'm describing here has been formerly known as psychopathic personality. That was changed to sociopath, so at this time probably it would have been more appropriate to say that what I'm talking about is a sociopathic disorder."

"Is that what Mr. Mays had?" Blakely asked, opening his eyes wider.

"Yeah," Groff answered. There was a silence, a long pause.

Later in his deposition, Groff made an important point. "It is very common," he said, "to have a child who is being abused who will not be critical of the abuser. I mean, it's not only common, but we know it as the Stockholm phenomena . . . For example, hostages are taken. After a period of time they actually begin to identify with the people who have been harming them the most and will actually say things in their favor. So even while Kimberly's actually telling me of what he really did, she's protective in saying these things." Earlier Groff had touched on this trait: "She tended to be using the phenomenon known as 'Denial,' which means on an unconscious level she would say, 'Yes, he whipped me on the legs, but . . .'—then either she would make a protective statement like 'I deserved it' or 'but it didn't hurt me' or 'but I don't care.' When a child makes those kinds of statements and you see tears in her eyes, then you know that on an unconscious level she's being protective of the person who is doing that to her." Groff said of Kimberly's protectiveness of Bob, "I would almost call it pathological bonding."

After five more months of delay, with Stephen Groff's deposition before the judge, a custody trial was finally scheduled for July 13, 1992.

On June 20, 1992, under the severe stress of preparing for the trial, Regina Twigg blew an aneurysm. The temporal artery that burst in her head almost killed her. After surgery, three days in intensive care, and several blood transfusions, she slowly began to stabilize. When her doctors requested that the custody trial be postponed, the judge removed the date from his calendar and once again ordered more mediation. No new trial date has been set as of this writing.

Discovering that they had lost their biological daughter was horror enough. Understanding now that she has been treated badly by a man who will not permit them even to see her is still worse.

Kimberly is trapped, caught somewhere between the emotional bonds established during the short lifetime she has spent with Bob Mays and the strong biological blood bond she shares with the Twiggs. She has already had three substitute mothers and lost two of them.

Legally the Twiggs could go and physically remove Kimberly from Bob Mays's home. They are her parents. She was wrongfully taken from them. They never relinquished her for adoption.

It is only their profound respect for Kimberly's conflict that has kept them from doing this. Sometimes they wonder if it is really in her best interest. There is no legal or emotional precedent for what they are facing—only the biblical story of the most ancient of recorded custody cases. Rather than cut her child in half, the real mother told King Solomon to let it stay with the wrong parent. Unfortunately Kimberly's is neither a biblical story nor a fairy tale. It is every parent's nightmare, and so far no King Solomon has emerged to set things right.

John Blakely estimates that a final judicial answer is still several years away. By the time the courts rule on custody and that ruling is appealed by the losing party, first at the Florida court level and then at the Supreme Court level, Kimberly, who is now fourteen, may well be an adult.

Chapter 38

The Last Word

On June 7, 1991, Ernest and Regina Twigg accepted a $7 million settlement from Hardee Memorial Hospital's compensation fund. The bulk of it is to be distributed to them monthly over the course of their lives. Beyond the obvious victory, there was vindication. The hospital had finally acknowledged the horrendous injustice that had been done to them.

Money has made life easier for the Twiggs. They still do not live luxuriously. They had struggled too long to ever do that. But Ernest has retired from his job as an Amtrak ticket clerk, and they finally have a house large enough for all of their children, including a bedroom set aside and waiting for Kimberly.

Regina is still very much as she always was. She still worries about money and spends it very carefully. A few days after the settlement was awarded she was scheduled to do housework for an elderly neighbor. Not wanting to let the woman down, she kept that job. The only difference was that after eight hours of cleaning, she refused to accept the $40 payment. "It's a gift," she said.

Bob Mays sued the hospital for $10 million. Attorneys Deborah Blue and William Partridge began preparing to defend against his suit in federal court. They considered trying to demonstrate that Mays was not an injured party since he, after all, ended up with a healthy, beautiful daughter. They were also expected to try to prove that the baby swap was indeed intentional, in which case, under Florida law, they would not be responsible for reparations.

Then, in July 1992, Hardee Memorial Hospital declared bankruptcy. It cited the baby swap as one of the major factors and closed its doors. On September 21, 1992, the hospital and the Florida Patients Compensation Fund agreed to pay $6.6 million to Robert and Kimberly Mays. The payments will be distributed over their lifetimes.

"I hope that the federal case will still go forward," hospital attorney William Partridge told me just days before the Mays settlement. "I hope that there will still be a trial and there will still be a jury. We need a trial to deal with the concept of an intentional swap. Finally, after all these years, we need to have somebody explain to a jury how those two babies got switched at birth. Someone needs to provide a logical explanation for all the bits and pieces that point to a baby swap conspiracy. We need a satisfactory resolution."

"It's about time we all found out," Regina Twigg said, squinting as the sun dried her tears. "It's about time, don't you think?"

Now, that may never happen.

The time had come when I decided that I had to go back to Florida and try once more to ferret out what had really happened in Hardee Memorial Hospital thirteen years earlier.

On December 10, 1991, I traveled to Hardee County, this time with a former cop who is the best private detective I know. The methods of investigative reporters and private detectives are often similar. We learn from each other. Skip Gochenour was also able to provide a measure of physical protection I thought I might need.

Researching and piecing together fragments of information so many years after an event is difficult at best, especially when the records have been altered and purged.

When addressed with conflicting information or allegations about the switch, I have tried to contact and speak to everyone involved.

We found Kathryn Drevermann, the Circle K employee who claimed a nurse's aide had confessed to her. She was living with her husband and children in a small modest house on a deserted back road in the tiny central Florida town of Zolfo Springs. Ray worked for a John Deere tractors dealer. Kathryn worked for Sunshine Foliage. They were plain-spoken, quiet people, unused to a lot of attention, and they were scared.

Kathryn and I had talked by phone several times, and she had grown to trust me. Ray opened the door and greeted us. We walked through the living room, past the paintings of Elvis Presley that hung above the couch, into the small, clean kitchen where doughnuts and coffee were waiting. We sat around the table until late into the night and talked.

"When my wife first came home four years ago all upset and told me what happened," Ray Drevermann said, half kidding, "I said, shut your damn mouth. Things can happen, and look, I was right. For years we didn't hear a word from anyone. But now all of a sudden the whole damn world's coming down on us!"

I explained to them that I was responsible for starting all this up again. I had gotten hold of Ray Starr's report and taped interviews that had been buried for nearly three years in a file drawer in a back room in John Blakely's office. Since

Blakely was not preparing a criminal case, one of his legal assistants, looking only for medical negligence leads, had discarded the material. I showed it to Blakely, and in the overriding interest of finding the truth, I decided to notify the hospital's attorneys, who had their own staff of private investigators.

Once the hospital and press became aware of Kathryn's story, she was besieged with calls from the media. She and Ray had also been followed by a bald-headed man with a .357 magnum.

"I seen the bullets in his truck," Ray told me. "First, I heard he was riding around town asking people where I lived, then circling my house real slow. One day I seen him following me. I pulled him over and said, 'Hey man, what's going on here?' 'Keep an eye on your wife,' he told me. 'There's ten million dollars involved.' He offered us protection. Turned out he worked for the hospital. They had sent him to track us down. All they had was your lead," he said looking at me. "They didn't know where we lived."

Next Kathryn got a call from Deborah Blue, who represented the hospital. "She's a fancy lady," Ray told me, "about thirty-five, maybe thirty-eight, with a red plaid dress on, red pantyhose, red high heels, and short, chopped-off blond hair. Her partner, another lawyer, a small skinny guy named Partridge or something, was with her. They took us to Hardee House for lunch. They said they had questioned Dr. Palmer and his attorney, and he was real nervous. They wanted us to ride in their car with them. Kathy told her what had happened when Patsy Webb came into the Circle K and said she switched them babies' bands. Deborah Blue began to shiver. She said a chill went down her back. They wanted to know who else Kathy had told. They was concerned in the restaurant that people would hear us."

Kathryn was able to confirm from memory everything she

had told private detective Ray Starr four years earlier. She was also able to describe the car to me, an old dark green Ford Galaxie, and the place where Patsy Webb was rumored to be living in a run-down cottage high in the winding country hills several miles from the store.

Stopping from time to time to ask directions at stores and houses, Skip Gochenour and I eventually tracked Patsy down. With geese honking in the yard and nipping at our heels and dogs barking loudly and chasing us, we finally found her, bedridden and hooked up to an oxygen tank in a small cluttered room that was lined with guns.

We introduced ourselves and asked her if she remembered the babies. She began to motion frantically. We looked around and saw that Skip was inadvertently standing on the tubes that led from the oxygen tank to her lungs. "Damn, Patsy, I'm sorry. I sure didn't mean to pressure you that way," he said, falling all over his shined leather shoes.

At first she told us she had nothing to say. We hung around and continued to make small talk. "Yes," she finally admitted, breathing with difficulty. "I still remember them babies. I remember the one with the bad heart, because it would get blue on you. You could tell just to look at it that it was sick."

When I asked her directly if she knew who had switched the babies' bands, her thin lips stretched tight across her gums. She shook her head, her dark eyes darted from side to side. "I can't say too much," she said. "It's water under the bridge. Besides, if it was me, I wouldn't admit it now. If I did it, you know, I wouldn't admit it."

We found Polly Rhodes, the elderly nurse's aide who said she had originally been scheduled to work the late shift on the night of the switch. She was also confined, but able to walk a little. Starved for company, she welcomed us. She invited us in, gave us gifts of crocheted crosses that she was making for her church and eagerly talked about everything except the baby switch. She told us that she is still in regular contact with Dena Spieth, Dr. Palmer and Velma Coker. "I have my ideas," she said over and over, "but I can't say nothing, and I don't want nobody to get in trouble."

When it was time to leave, Gochenour asked if there was anything we could do for her. "Would you mind being a good boy," she said, "and running over to the Circle K to get me a Slurpee?"

"With pleasure," he said.

She smiled coquettishly, revealing her pink toothless gums.

"I've got my ideas," she repeated while he was gone. "Honey, I know who done it, but I just can't say."

The next evening Gochenour and I visited the hospital attorneys and shared our latest findings with them. We sat around for hours with Deborah Blue and her colleague Bill Partridge. Ray Drevermann was right. She was fancy, all dressed up in a white suit and black silk blouse. She was also funny, smart, hard-driving and determined to get to the bottom of the case. As the night wore on and we all relaxed, she kicked off her black high-heels, threw her long shapely legs over her desk and swore in a deceptively laid-back Southern drawl that she would get to the bottom of this even if it was the last thing she did.

The next day I knocked on Dena Spieth's door. There was no answer. I returned several times. She was away in Nevada visiting her children. When reached later by phone she refused to consider that Ernest Palmer may have been involved in the switch. "I am absolutely in love with Dr. Palmer," she said. "We all are. He's a good Christian man. He would not have ordered those babies switched. I think Johns Hopkins Hospital was wrong. I do not think there was a switch at all. I truthfully believe that Kimberly was raised by her father."

Before leaving Hardee County we tracked down Barbara's

mother, Velma Coker. She turned pale and began to tremble when we walked into her Project Hope office and introduced ourselves. "I have nothing to say to either of you," she said.

"Mrs. Coker," Gochenour said, "before we go I have just one question. Shortly before her death, do you recall ever taking your daughter Barbara Mays to Regina Twigg's house to see her baby daughter? Do you recall looking at Arlena through the screened-in porch?"

Velma Coker's respiration rate changed. She began to tremble visibly.

"Absolutely not," she said. "I've never seen Mrs. Twigg in my entire life and I hope I never will."

Soon after I returned home, Kathryn Drevermann called to say that the hospital had sent her a sworn statement to sign. It said, in part, "Mrs. Webb advised that she knew about the switch and in fact had been involved in the switch. Mrs. Webb further advised that her involvement in the switch was at the direction of Dr. Ernest Palmer. Mrs. Webb further stated that the Twiggs should 'leave well enough alone.' Mrs. Webb described the motive for the switch as being that the Mayses were unable to have a healthy baby." Kathryn, who the hospital believes is an entirely credible witness with no motive for lying, swore that the statement was true and signed it.

Patsy Webb gasped for breath when I called her recently to tell her about Kathryn Drevermann's sworn statement. "She's a damn liar," Patsy snapped.

"Why would Kathryn lie?" Raymond Drevermann asked. "She has nothing to gain from this. All she has is people following her and threatening her. She never asked Patsy Webb to come into that store. She never went to anyone and told them. You all came to her. All she did was tell the truth. Sometimes the truth hurts."

"Yes ma'am," Cindy Bishop, Kathy Drevermann's former boss at the Circle K, said, "I do recall Kathryn was upset one morning. She told me a sick lady had been in the store—very agitated—and stayed there for a while and talked, but I can't recall any of the details. It was a long, long time ago."

"I recall Kathy coming over to my house and talking about the baby switch," Gail Bandy, Kathy's sister-in-law, said shyly. "She said the lady told her Dr. Palmer gave her the order to switch those bands." Kathy's mama had been there too. "I wish she was still alive to tell you. She was real upset by it; she kept on saying somebody ought to know about this, somebody ought to know. We all think Mama had a hand in calling the police department and getting that detective, Ray Starr, involved. Mama had friends there."

Taking the phone from her sister-in-law, Kathryn added, "People are threatening me and my children. It's lucky my husband and I are volunteer rescue workers and firefighters. He rides with the police on weekends; the police here are our friends. Since all these threats started, they've been watching over us; we've got young ones of our own to protect."

After talking to Patsy Webb and Kathryn Drevermann, I decided to try to reach Dr. Palmer one last time. "Our attorney, Mr. Somers, has advised my husband not to make any statements," Ernest Palmer's wife said. "I personally think it was a terrible, horrible human error, just a tragedy. It's real bad for a dedicated physician like my husband, who has given his entire life to medicine, to have to go through this." I could hear the pain in Mrs. Palmer's voice as I thanked her and told her I would contact her attorney.

"Dr. Palmer categorically denies any knowledge of this switch," Clifford Somers said from his office in Tampa when I asked him about Kathryn Drevermann's sworn statement. "I have represented a lot of people, and I can tell you he is one of the most decent men I have ever known. This is all so sick. He did not know anything about it. This is just plain simply not true."

Throughout the three-year period that I worked on this

book, I repeatedly attempted to speak with Bob Mays, and I was repeatedly turned down. In May 1992, I received a letter from one of his attorneys asking to review my manuscript before publication. I declined the request and asked again to interview Mr. Mays so I could publish his side of the story.

On August 18, 1992, I received a collect call from Arthur Ginsberg. He had finally agreed to be interviewed on Robert Mays's behalf. "I don't really have a theory about how the switch occurred, unless it happened when the babies were being bathed," he said. "But I do know that Bob Mays had nothing to do with it."

Ginsberg flatly denied the truth of all of Cindy Tanner Mays's statements about Bob Mays's temper, his abusive treatment of Kimberly, his drinking and the episode with the gun. "I've known Bob for four years. There's no indication of a violent temper or any of the rest of it." Ginsberg added that Bob's refusal to let Cindy see Kim was a "smart move," and said that seeing Regina Twigg is not in Kimberly's best interest. He described a report by a court-appointed psychologist suggesting that Regina herself needed therapy. Perhaps Kimberly could see Ernest, he conceded, but not unsupervised, "because Ernest is a vehicle of Regina."

Not long ago, a new witness surfaced. Virginia Jones is a licensed practical nurse. At the time of the switch she says she was visiting her sick mother at Hardee Memorial Hospital. Because the hospital was short of beds, Virginia's mother was being cared for on the maternity floor. Each day as she visited, she stopped at the nursery window and admired the two babies. On December 5, the day of Regina Twigg's and Barbara Mays's discharge, she arrived early. As she approached the hospital, she says, she saw a nurse run out into the parking area with a baby in her arms. The nurse gave the baby to someone in a waiting car and said, "Get the hell out of here as fast as you can."

Virginia Jones claims that as a religious person she had to come forward. She could no longer live with the guilt of keeping this information to herself. Since the revelation, she has been besieged with anonymous threats. At least, she says, her conscience is clear.

So many years have passed. No one can say for certain why Kimberly has had three mothers or how she ended up with the wrong parents. What can be said, however, with great certainty, is that it was not an accident. Four Ident-a-bands were switched on two infants at the same time. It was a premeditated act. We may never know by whom.

Is it possible that Barbara Mays, overcome with grief after learning that her child had a serious congenital heart defect, walked into the nursery and switched the bands without ever telling anyone what she had done? Is it possible that a doctor, either for money or with misguided altruism, arranged the switch? Is it possible that Bob Mays and Barbara Mays together came up with a plan? Is it possible that Velma Coker, wanting to ease her daughter's loss, sought the help of hospital employees?

Is it possible that, in a moment of weakness, an aide told a total stranger how the switch really occurred?

There will always be the possibility of new litigation and more new witnesses and leads. As long as there is money to pay them, there will be lawyers, private investigators and psychiatrists on both sides. Since there is no federal statute of limitations on kidnapping there may even still be convictions and prison sentences. Unfortunately, while the court battles rage on, the years roll by. What remains of Kimberly's childhood will soon be gone. A little girl's chance to share growing up with her family will soon be lost forever. Beyond judicial rulings, monetary compensation and ultimate culpability, that is the bottom line.

"Kimberly is my daughter," Regina says sadly. "She is my lost treasure, the baby that was literally stolen from my womb. Nothing can change that. As long as I live I will love her and continue to pray that someday she will come home."

ABOUT THE AUTHOR

LORETTA SCHWARTZ-NOBEL numbers among her honors the Columbia School of Journalism Award, the Robert F. Kennedy Award, the Women in Communications Award, the American Bar Association Award, the Penny Missouri Award, and the National Society of Professional Journalists Award. A resident of Gladwyne, Pennsylvania, she authored *A Mother's Story: The Truth About the Baby M Case, Starving in the Shadow of Plenty,* and the Edgar-nominated true-crime work *Engaged to Murder.* She is working on the forthcoming *Forsaking All Others: The Betty Broderick Story.*